"This extraordinary book plumbs the de,
kept secrets: gratitude. Intellectually satisfying, spiritually
edifying, and profoundly personal, Charles Shelton provides a
wise and compassionate analysis of what has been often
referred to as the 'greatest of the virtues.' Wisdom bursts forth
from every page. Read it and savor it over and over again.
You will be deeply fulfilled and overwhelmingly grateful. I
know I was."

—Robert A. Emmons, PhD, professor of psychology;
editor-in-chief, *The Journal of Positive Psychology*

"There is no emotion more central to Christian spirituality
than gratitude, and Charles Shelton discusses it in this book
with theological and psychological insight."

—Rev. John I. Jenkins, CSC
President, University of Notre Dame

"As the coach of a successful program, I feel most grateful for
the many opportunities I have had over the years to influence
the lives of numerous student athletes. Charles Shelton's book
on gratitude provides me many insights into, and personal
understanding of, the gratitude I feel. *The Gratitude Factor*
offers a wonderful overview of gratitude's role in fostering
healthy living and life satisfaction. The practical exercises and
strategies for fostering gratitude will enable every reader not
only to experience more richly the gratitude he or she feels,
but also to share that gratitude with others."

—Mike Krzyzewski
Head coach, men's basketball, Duke University

"In *The Gratitude Factor*, Shelton shows us, both spiritually and
psychologically, the value of gratitude for our own lives.
Drawing on the spiritual tradition of St. Ignatius Loyola and
using exercises and reflective questions interspersed throughout
each chapter, Shelton invites the reader to understand the
gratitude research through our own experience. I promise that
as you read this book, you will find yourself being grateful."

—David L. Fleming, SJ, editor, *Review for Religious*;
author of *What Is Ignatian Spirituality?*

The
Gratitude
Factor

The Gratitude Factor

Enhancing Your Life through Grateful Living

CHARLES M. SHELTON, PHD

HiddenSpring

Imprimi potest
Rev. Douglas W. Marcouiller, SJ
Provincial, Missouri Province of the Society of Jesus
October 21, 2009

Cover design by Joy Taylor
Book design by Lynn Else

Library of Congress Cataloging-in-Publication Data

Shelton, Charles M.
    The gratitude factor : enhancing your life through grateful living / Charles M. Shelton.
        p. cm.
    Includes bibliographical references.
    ISBN 978-1-58768-063-2 (alk. paper)
    1. Gratitude—Religious aspects—Christianity. I. Title.
    BV4647.G8S54 2010
    241´.4—dc22

                                                                                    2010021741

Published by HiddenSpring
An imprint of Paulist Press
997 Macarthur Boulevard
Mahwah, New Jersey 07430

www.hiddenspringbooks.com

Printed and bound in the
United States of America

CONTENTS

For Michael D. Barber, SJ, and
John K. Ridgway, SJ—both
brothers and friends—always grateful

INTRODUCTION

"For me, I think of gratitude as a lollipop bursting apart,
spreading sweetness everywhere the parts land."
                    —Answer of an artist to the question:
                         "What is your image of gratitude?"

*G*ratitude is one of life's essential ingredients. Whether reminiscing on the past, considering our existing situation, or focusing on fleeting thoughts or vivid memories, we know that opportunities for gratitude abound. In fact, just reading the words on this page affords a moment for gathering memories that warm the heart. Far too frequently, however, gratitude's many invitations are taken for granted or ignored. Sadly and far too willingly (indeed, seemingly effortlessly), we erect barriers even to recognizing the opportunities when gratitude beckons. We can choose to decline its invitation, and unfortunately we do so all too often. Whether it be a lack of focus that diverts us, a specific event that distracts us, or a mood that seizes us, we frequently create obstacles to living life gratefully.

I write this book as a Jesuit psychologist, and both of these features (first, as a Jesuit, and second, as a psychologist) have helped to shape the thoughts contained in the pages that follow. As a Jesuit priest I have been blessed with numerous experiences that have led me to feel the gratitude I write about. Moreover, for St. Ignatius, the founder of the Jesuits, gratitude was a defining feature for one's relationship with God. In his view, gratitude was an essential and readily observable feature of a grace-filled life. Likewise, the field of psychology elaborates many ideas in the pages ahead. Stated simply, having a grateful outlook is one of the best investments we can make for ensuring the happy, healthy lives we desire. This is something that psychological science has confirmed. Throughout this book I draw upon my training as a clinical psychologist to provide engaging questions, instructive strategies, and practical exercises to increase grateful living.

Speaking personally, I was surprised to discover that the greatest joy in writing this book was the gratitude evoked when I spoke with friends, colleagues, and strangers regarding their own ideas about, and experiences of, gratitude. When appropriate, I draw upon the stories and words from people ranging in age from their early twenties to mid-eighties to add flavor and depth to the ideas offered in the following pages.

As any reader knows, at the beginning of a book the author frequently pauses to thank the many individuals who in one way or another helped in shaping ideas, presenting them, or serving as personal supports that sustained the author's project; that is, when listing the contributions of others, authors reveal their gratitude. That having been said, this written undertaking affords me one advantage: My gratefulness toward those who in one way or another helped in my efforts comes with ease, and with the topic itself being that of "gratitude," pointing out those supportive individuals becomes an effortless undertaking. Starkly stated, I've been spoiled!

I owe a special debt of thanks to Bob Emmons, professor of psychology at the University of California, Davis. Though Bob would humbly deny it, he is without doubt the country's leading academic researcher on gratitude. His faithful responses to my e-mails and his always-insightful comments, not to mention his guiding hand in steering me to numerous references and resources, have led to a significantly better book. The Jesuit community at Regis University, Denver, was always supportive and took a more-than-active interest in this writing venture. The players on the soccer and baseball teams at Regis University, for whom I serve as chaplain, have never failed in being significant sources for my gratitude with their smiles, determination, and good cheer, not to mention their devotion to their sports. They not only keep me "young at heart," but their youthful enthusiasm offered a natural laboratory to observe gratitude in action.

I am gratefully indebted to the Nemec family, which considers me one of their own. In a similar way, the "McGann Clan" makes the experience of gratitude on my part delightful. Likewise, I will always be grateful to Angie and Steve Potter and their children for making me an "honorary Potter." The Pattridge, Scarth, Young, Van Natter, and Weber families have always been close to my heart as well. Many former students whose weddings I witnessed have graciously allowed me to be "Uncle Charlie" (and now "Grandpa Charlie!") to their children, and for this I am always grateful. Millie Sperlak, unbeknown to her, became for me a constant model of grateful living just by her presence and good heart. The same is true of Mary Stegeman, who has always shown me kindness and generosity. Dick Campbell has always shown interest in my work and has been a source of encouragement. Matt Hogan, Jerry Rouse, Sr. Corita Hoffman, OSB, and Paul Vu, SJ, were always good sounding boards, who shared with me their own thoughts on gratitude.

My sisters Lois Jansen and Marty Shelton and their families have always displayed for me gratitude's unfolding features. My mom, June Shelton, showed me how to grow gratefully in one's later years. She and my dad, Walter Shelton, both now deceased, modeled for me that kindness is truly possible (and attainable) in a life we all find too short. I will forever be indebted to them for planting in me the seeds that over the years have allowed gratitude to bloom.

Last, I dedicate this book to my two closest Jesuit friends, Mike Barber, SJ, and John Ridgway, SJ. Over the past few decades they have proven and remain today two of the best sources for cultivating within me the grateful life. My ongoing friendship with each unfailingly provides me the continual reminder that because of my friendship with them, there always lies before me an invitation to gratitude.

Charles Shelton, PhD
Department of Psychology, Regis University

Chapter One

WHY GRATITUDE?

When he was very little, my grandson had one of the worst
types of epilepsy imaginable. We sought the advice of numerous
specialists but didn't know what would happen. Fortunately,
everything turned out all right, but there were so many
moments of fear and uncertainty. Several years later we were
planning a visit to our son and his family and, while there, to
celebrate my birthday. Before we left I was talking to him on
the phone and in the middle of the conversation my grandson
got on the line. He calls me "Gumpy." He is learning to play the
piano and he told me, "When you come, I'm going to play
Happy Birthday, Gumpy." Well, you know what? We visited
them and my grandson played that song and didn't miss a note.
Talk about gratitude! It brought tears to my eyes.

—A grandparent describing a personal experience of gratitude

The other day an incoming e-mail containing numerous gratitude
statements caught my attention. One went something like this: "Be
thankful that an alarm clock wakes you because it shows you are
alive." Another example: "Be grateful even if the meal you fix fails
to turn out as you expect, because it shows you have enough to eat."
Another illustration is helpful and yet annoying: "Be grateful even
when you are short of electricity or have higher electric bills, because
it demonstrates you at least possess the means to live comfortably."
Finally, an example that might prove especially useful to remember
around the middle of April: "When paying income taxes, don't focus
on what you might have to give, but on what you already have." It
makes sense, since paying taxes demonstrates some or all of the following: a job, money in the bank, investments on which to draw on,
or some source of income. For sure, slicing off the gratitude rationale
for each statement makes for a distressing thought. And rightly so!

1

Who wants to be stuck with higher bills or more taxes? Nonetheless, these statements point out that there is usually a deeper truth to most of our daily experiences than we typically consider. When we link each statement with some notion of thanks, a welcome insight surfaces that not only enhances mood but also provides a new pair of glasses (an appreciative lens) through which to eye our world. In sum, gratitude alters our outlook, and this newly discovered perspective proves both meaningful and fun.

Gratitude is infectious and its sources numerous. It flows from thoughts, whether random or profound. It originates from actions ranging from the exciting to the commonplace. It is a link to other emotions such as joy, surprise, and contentment, but it also finds a home with sorrow or grief. Gratitude flows from, among other things, ordinary moments, distant memories, surprising intrusions, unexpected insights, personal struggles, and the discovery of the unknown. People's personal comments highlighted in the chapters ahead verify that the origins of gratitude are not only many, but seeded within virtually all human experiences.

Definition of Gratitude

America's emphasis on gratitude has been characterized as a saving grace. Despite daily doses of disturbing headlines, Americans consider themselves a grateful lot. Most people regularly report thoughts or expressions of thankfulness. For most Americans, gratitude resides in family, health, children, a spouse, life itself, freedom, and God.[1]

These findings are hardly surprising. Moments of thanksgiving are woven abundantly through America's past. Early in its history, hopeful immigrants (those shackled as slaves being the notable exception) fled homelands in search of a safe haven to express their ideas, to enhance their liberties, and to fulfill their dreams—in short, to begin life anew.[2] All in all, given their motives and hopes, it can be said that newcomers to America were primed for gratitude! Achieving their goals came at significant cost, however. For many, the American journey to freedom was a checkered one; frequently a slow if not a painful road. Even today, many struggle to attain the economic means most citizens take for granted.³ Yet Americans' fondness for gratitude endures. Generation after generation of immigrants adopted a country whose increasingly expanding political reach and plentiful natural resources enabled them to carve out a life that never ceased to sow the seeds of gratitude. Still today, when reading the occasional newspaper story of immigrants becoming naturalized citizens, we see their quoted, heartfelt expressions of "thanks" as simply continuing a tradition of gratitude springing from previous generations and centuries. In a sense, the American experiment *is* the American dream fulfilled: a seemingly limitless testing ground offering opportunities for grateful expression.

Early American settlers expressed their gratitude by borrowing from Native American rituals and incorporating them into European customs and prayers. In the early 1620s Native Americans and the Pilgrims celebrated the harvest by sharing meals together. An early observance of gratitude occurred on July 8, 1630, when the Massachusetts Bay Colony celebrated its first Thanksgiving. What was on the minds of early Pilgrims who had risked everything to embark upon such an unknown future? Suffering for weeks through perilous ocean journeys, jammed into boats, and all too often witnessing firsthand sickness, disease, and death, they placed themselves in a situation in which they were facing as much uncertainty about the present as they did about their future. Moreover, settling in a new land forced them to contend with additional hardships. Living conditions were appalling. Merciless winters, inadequate shelter, widespread diseases, and frequently death itself became their unwelcome companions. Yet, in the midst of such overwhelming difficulties they persevered. Caught between a past they left behind and an uncertain and ominous future, they discovered the need to offer thanks. Over time, public expressions of gratitude evolved into an enduring American theme. This historical unfolding surfaced at Valley Forge, followed, in turn, by Washington's "Presidential Proclamation Number One," which he issued shortly after his inauguration. Decades later, Lincoln's declaration in the midst of the wrenching years of the Civil War focused the nation's attention on the need for thanksgiving. Building on this tradition, presidents since Lincoln have offered statements expressing gratitude for America's bountiful riches. Perhaps Thanksgiving as a national holiday best summarizes our history.[4]

Free of the glitzy advertising that so surrounds Christmas festivities, Thanksgiving Day becomes a time for genuine and heartfelt thanks. The television host Oprah Winfrey writes in the magazine bearing her name, "Thanksgiving is one of the best times to share what you know to be true....This season don't get lost in making the perfect meal or become overwhelmed with all the folks in your house. Use this time to center yourself in a lasting sense of gratitude. Accept with an open heart whatever is going on in your life right now. And, whenever you can't think of something to be grateful for, remember your breath."[5] Adds one religious leader, "During Thanksgiving week, when I think about life and about lives, I am much more inclined to want to celebrate than to analyze, to smile than to cry, to give thanks for what is and for what has been rather than to complain about what hasn't been or won't be anymore."[6] As a way of summary, in the first Thanksgiving that Peter Jennings celebrated after becoming a United States citizen, the late ABC news anchor captured the spirit of the holiday's ideals when he remarked, "Every fourth Thursday of November, I have given thanks, because America has been everything I hoped it to be."[7]

In addition to what is said above, Thanksgiving also shifts our perspective. Like most holidays, it becomes a day of remembrance of things past. In November, newspapers, television shows, and sermons remind us of the trials and fortitude of our forefathers during our nation's infancy. But like many annually celebrated events, it is also a source for highly cherished personal memories. For example, an older woman wrote about her difficult surgery performed years earlier to correct a potentially crippling condition. She described the success of the surgery and the care and well wishes she received from friends during her recovery. Toward the end of her story she recounted the effect of an upcoming Thanksgiving celebration. "I remember Thanksgiving Day that year—about three and a half months after surgery. I was so overwhelmed by gratitude that tears flowed freely. I really couldn't find words to express adequately what I was feeling. I just knew God's loving, healing presence in a very personal way." When all the above is taken together, it is not far-fetched to conclude that a sense of gratitude seems to course through our country's veins.

All the same, America hardly stands alone when it comes to celebrating gratitude. The Center for World Thanksgiving in Dallas points out that, although Thanksgiving Day is rooted deep in the American tradition, many other cultures, too, have kindled the theme of thanksgiving. A number of Asian and South American countries celebrate gratitude through various customs, observances, rituals, and prayers. Indeed, in addition to the United States, several other countries have officially set aside a day of national Thanksgiving.[8]

Why Study Gratitude?

Why write about gratitude? A more appropriate question might be: Is there a more enjoyable topic to discuss or focus on? Reflecting on moments when we feel grateful and calling to mind savored memories that flood us with a sense of awe and appreciation make gratitude a subject definitely worth pursuing. As an additional benefit, gratitude is associated with and influences a wide range of emotional experiences and behaviors that together promote positive growth and healthy development. At the same time, the fast-paced and stress-filled lives of many Americans erect continual roadblocks to living life gratefully.

To sharpen our focus, let's spell out a number of factors that highlight the benefits of and challenges to living gratefully in twenty-first-century America.

GRATITUDE ENRICHES LOVE

As a clinical psychologist I have been privileged to walk with others when they have expressed feelings ranging from grief and darkest despair to consolation and heartfelt joy. Naturally, my own life, too, has reflected the joys, sorrows, frustrations, and hopes that go with being human. Loving relationships are essential ingredients for a healthy and a whole life. Yet, these cherished relationships leave us incomplete. Stated differently, if we focus only on love, we fail to draw forth from the loves of our lives their fullest potential. More than likely, our personal lives and love itself are short-changed.

Gratitude enables us to savor and relish our loves. To illustrate, pause for a moment and bring to mind someone you love deeply. After spending several moments feeling your love for this person, shift your focus to a sense of gratitude for this person's presence in your life. Now spend a few moments just being with the gratitude you feel. Now ask yourself: What would my love be like if I did not have gratitude for this person? When we become *consciously* grateful for the loves that our hearts cherish, then love flourishes; in fact, we come to experience love in a new way. Gratitude transforms love's quality. When loving others, we are most true to our humanity, but when loving with gratitude, we come to know love in its fullest expression. When loving gratefully, we treasure our lives and the lives of others as gifts, tapping increasingly (and more effortlessly) into the insights that love and gratitude offer.

GRATITUDE IS A POSITIVE EXPERIENCE

A second reason for studying gratitude lies in its positive effects. Survey after survey documents the fact that grateful people are happy people.[9] In a Gallup Poll of "American teens and adults, over 90% of respondents indicated that expressing gratitude helped them to feel 'extremely happy' or 'somewhat happy.'"[10] Indeed, the English writer G. K. Chesterton noted that from gratitude are derived "the most purely joyful moments that have been known to man."[11] As I discussed this topic with others over the years, I was struck by the positive feelings it triggered. When interviewing people about gratitude, the conversations uplifted both of us. Frequently, after finishing the discussion, one or both of us commented on the joy we felt. Never before had I studied a subject that generated such a wealth of positive consequences. To illustrate, walking across campus last week, I was stopped by a colleague who shared with me the reactions of a group of health-care professionals to a speech she had given the previous week. The turmoil in health care today meant that many in the audience would be discouraged. Coincidentally, several weeks earlier I had interviewed her for this gratitude study. That conversation, she told me, led her to make gratitude the theme of her talk. This speech on the topic of gratitude, she stated, a surprise to conference participants, was received quite favorably. However, despite this example, I wish to avoid the perception that everything about gratitude is positive. As the following chapters show, gratitude is a complex subject. Having stated this caution, we nonetheless can explore enthusiastically its many-sided facets.

GRATITUDE HELPS COMMUNITIES AS WELL AS INDIVIDUALS

The benefits of gratitude go beyond individuals. "It is hard to conceive of a human society in which gratitude and its consequences do not play important social roles."[12] For society to flourish, cherished attitudes such as helping those in need and showing concern for others require encouragement. This goal, of course, is more easily said than done. With over three hundred million people, Americans obviously lack both the desire and the means for intimacy with all but the smallest fraction of their fellow citizens and, therefore, choose to reserve their time for family, friends, and valued colleagues. Given the diversity of peoples and perspectives, the possibility for misunderstanding looms high.

In a similar vein, when we live fast-paced and highly stressed lives, considerable effort is required to focus awareness on the needs and concerns of those in the wider community. Thus, with such a highly diverse population and with the time-crunching pace of modern life, it is reasonable to encourage some minimal standards as a way to forge some common bonds that Americans can agree on and endorse. Likely candidates for what might be characterized as a common morality include staying active in civic affairs (such as voting), volunteering resources or time for projects that benefit others, restraining aggression, adopting a basic respect toward the ideas held by others (with no obligation to agree with them and the distinct right to disagree), and viewing others as individuals who possess moral dignity (a personal conscience) that requires us, even in the midst of disagreement, to refrain from humiliating them.

Developing these common standards for morality is increasingly important, for as one leading educator notes:

> During most of the twentieth century, first artists and intellectuals, then broader segments of the society, chal-

lenged every convention, every prohibition, every regulation that cramped the human spirit or blocked its appetite and ambitions. Today, a reaction has set in, born of a recognition that the public needs common standards to hold a diverse society together, to prevent ecological disaster, to maintain confidence in government, to conserve scarce resources, to escape disease, to avoid the inhumane applications of technology.[13]

How might gratitude benefit a common morality? As previously noted, the emotional experience of gratitude evokes positive feelings. Further, when feeling grateful or having other positive emotions, we are frequently inclined to behave in a more caring manner. All in all, when we feel it, we are more apt to show it![14] As a consequence, relationships are strengthened and ties to the wider community, enhanced. Truly, it is not an exaggeration to say that "gratitude is one of the building blocks of a civil and humane society."[15] As such, its cultivation goes far in helping promote the common good.

Besides serving in some measure as a catalyst for helping others, the presence of gratitude more than likely benefits the everyday lives of citizens. Take the average American citizen. Now, fill his or her life with gratitude. How do you envision that this person's reactions might be altered by a healthy dose of gratitude? It stands to reason that grateful citizens forge enduring bonds of concern among themselves and between themselves and government. In a free society, the appreciation that people express turns on its head the notion that people live lives only for themselves. Rather than narrowly focus on personal gain, thankful citizens would in all likelihood be sensitive to how the talents and presence of others in the wider American community promote the common good. Moreover, motivated by their gratitude, they would be more inclined to consider the needs of fellow citizens, thereby promoting a growing goodwill within and among communities. At the same time, people's appreciation would foster a broadened openness toward neighbors and other groups, and this, in the long run, strengthens democracy's vitality.

Despite the sometimes-heated debate about the proper role of government in American life, imagine what America would be like if each of its citizens was thankful for the vital role government provides, such as protection of its citizenry and the maintenance of everyday functions (for example, emergency services, waste management, and so on). For one, it would not take much argument to convince grateful citizens to get involved in civic affairs and to vote. In a country where typically less than half of the voting-age population casts their ballots, voter gratitude might just well be the healthy antidote to electoral apathy. Two, grateful citizens in all likelihood would be more law-abiding, more sensitive to the needs of the environment, and more willing to volunteer and take part in community affairs. Finally, Americans are tired of the shrill and negative tones that, sadly, seem to tarnish so many election campaigns, whether local, state, or national in scope. Injecting a healthy dose of gratitude into these contests would seem to benefit every voter and candidate.

GRATITUDE HELPS FIGHT NEGATIVITY

A critical reason for living life gratefully is to counter and halt the all-too-human tendency to slide into negativity. Humans often overemphasize negative and downplay positive events. "Research consistently shows that negative qualities often command more attention and seem more important than positive qualities."[16] We need not pause long to apprehend the truth of this statement. For example, if I put together a three-hour presentation for my colleagues and after the event seven participants offer positive feedback and one colleague criticizes my performance, whose response am I more likely to dwell on over the next few days? Like most people (assuming the respondents were sincere when offering their feedback), I am more susceptible to brooding over comments arising from the sole dissenting voice! A rational response? Probably not. Yet, we fret needlessly when receiving negative feedback. Another common example that demonstrates this bias toward negativity is anticipation around an upcoming event. For example, suppose I am looking forward to a vacation. I could spend time imagining what could go right. After all, I could enjoy myself or find myself pleasantly surprised. This response, however, is dwarfed by the numerous dire responses that vie for attention! Opportunities for worry are virtually limitless. To list just a few: first, I forget to pack everything I need; second, as a result of a car accident or traffic jam, I miss my plane; third, I get sick (or even worse, find myself a patient in the local hospital!); fourth, the weatherman's prediction for sunny skies proves woefully misguided and the outdoor concert I eagerly looked forward to is canceled; fifth, while I am away, my home is vandalized or someone I love falls ill. Humans nearly always generate more negative than positive responses.

All in all, disruptive experiences and feelings (for example, disappointment, emotional distress, sadness, grief, envy, and anger) can hijack our consciousness, thereby derailing focus and depleting psychic energy. The Dutch psychologist Nico Frijda wisely counsels that life lacks fairness, a truth we forget with apparent ease. As an example, fear might paralyze us for years, whereas the joy experienced when we are with a friend or the pride that flows from our achieving a goal quickly vanishes. Human beings, unfortunately, are prone to having negative emotions linger while positive ones evaporate.[17] Yet, even though this negativity bias exists, it need not imprison us. We can overcome the discouragements and concerns that negativity evokes, but to do so comes at a cost; it requires focused and consistent *effort*. We do possess the power to counter this negativity by summoning pleasant memories to mind and kindling thoughts that warm our heart and evoke gratitude for the many kindnesses shown us. Keeping all the above in mind, living life gratefully, though it takes persistent effort, remains an unfailing antidote to our natural tendency to succumb to the lures of negativity.

As an example, the following poignant story written by a middle-aged woman in crisis exhibits the power of gratitude in overcoming a profoundly negative state.

> It was a few days ago. I was depressed and very distressed. I was feeling somewhat suicidal. Things looked pretty bad, and I wasn't sure what to do or where to go. I have felt this way on many occasions. I tried the crisis line…on previous occasions. I called again that evening. I was fortunate enough to talk with a psych nurse.…She was so very kind and helpful to me. She was understanding, caring, and supportive. Even her tone of voice was comforting. We talked for a bit and she encouraged me to go home and call her back. I did that. I had started feeling less agitated and more hopeful. She said she wanted me to call her

again in the morning unless I needed to call back again in the middle of the night....I felt so much better....I am so very grateful to her for helping save my life. I thank God for her.

Because of this experience of gratitude, the question was then posed: "Did you notice any changes in yourself (for example, in attitudes, behaviors, or outlook)?" Her response proved simple yet elegant: "The experience was full of sadness and despair. But my hope was rekindled by this soft voice in the darkest of nights....She gave me dignity and showed compassion. The gratitude I feel toward her and the crisis line is immeasurable. I am better for it. I am alive."

Her gratitude was able to pierce the cloud of negativity manifested by her suicidal thinking. This woman's profoundly felt gratitude starkly illustrates the *potential* that gratitude offers as an ally in our struggles with negativity. And her response mirrors what the research says about gratitude. For example, millions of Americans are afflicted with mental illness, such as depression, anxiety, and addictions.[18] Yet, a factor consistently found to be associated with a reduced risk of having a mental disorder is possessing a sense of thankfulness.[19]

GRATITUDE RELIEVES STRESS

In light of the above, one factor that magnifies our focus on negative events is the stressful pace of modern life. Intensifying reactions of anger—even rage—are more and more common. Travelers endure the frustration of canceled flights and crowded planes and are exposed to air rage from other incensed passengers. Most drivers at one time or another have wondered if they will fall victim to road rage from an irate driver. Rudeness increasingly appears as the norm when working in offices, eating in restaurants, and shopping in stores. An evolving work environment that includes unrealistic expectations, job insecurity, and longer working hours has created "desk rage."[20] In the face of an ever-increasing amount of hassles, taking the time to cultivate a grateful spirit appears to offer a welcome antidote and a source for greater joy and contentment.[21]

But it is not only the incidents of stress in our lives that lead to problems; it is the time pressures that stress produces, such as the likes of an already jammed calendar. In a recent study on jobs and stress it was found that one-third of working Americans are chronically overworked, and nearly nine out of ten report that their work is so demanding that they don't have time to get everything done.[22] Balancing a frenzied work schedule, sustaining a network of valued relationships (which frequently include friends, children, a spouse, aging parents, siblings, and coworkers), and sorting through an ever-expanding information glut fueled by increasingly sophisticated forms of electronic gadgets and inventions, such as the Internet, text messaging, e-mail, voice mail, and faxes—creating a seemingly unending workday—all of these feel overwhelming at times. In order to negotiate this maze, individuals extract as much time as they can from daily schedules and, in the process, incur significant sleep debt. According to sleep experts, on any given day more than one hundred million Americans feel the stress associated with sleep deprivation.[23] Moreover, frenetic lifestyles and diminishing rest combine to drain our psyche's ability to cope with ever-burdening demands. As a consequence, many seek refuge in an autopilot mode of consciousness.[24] In its essence, autopilot consciousness blends routine and reaction with just enough psychic investment to accomplish goals and engage life meaningfully. Then, when confronted with an unanticipated event or crisis, we mobilize our energies and hone our focus in order to master whatever urgent concern has our attention. A two-career couple with children offers a fitting example. Both parents faithfully fulfill their obligations to work and home and, when necessary, respond immediately to any unexpected event (for example, suddenly realizing that their two children ages six and eight have simultaneous soccer games at opposite ends of town!). Both these adults live in a sort of autopilot mode as they preoccupy themselves with their roles and obligation.

Living day-to-day life in a mode of autopilot consciousness spawns a number of benefits.[25] These include making only minimal investment in some pursuits, thereby conserving psychic energies; successfully negotiating everyday concerns so as to provide a sense of order and manageability; and achieving the benefits of an uncluttered world to ensure security. In sum, autopilot consciousness allows us to successfully manage and master our everyday lives, like the parents above who divide up tasks and get their children to their games at scheduled times. However, a trade-off is required. Autopilot consciousness diminishes our capacity for solitude and contemplation, vital ingredients for personal growth. When this mode of consciousness takes increasing hold of daily life, we find ourselves with diminishing self-insight and perception. A frequent casualty of this narrowed focus is our *conscious* awareness of gratitude. In essence, an autopilot consciousness translates to a consciousness of routine that all too commonly ignores life's blessings. Attention to wonder, novelty, or surprise dims as we yield to a taken-for-granted existence. Over the course of the day, we grow so accustomed to ordinary events or are so absorbed in the moment that we fail to acknowledge blessings bestowed. (Pause to ask yourself, how often over the past twenty-four hours have you taken the time to feel truly thankful for your life and the many blessings and opportunities you have had, whether they be ordinary or significant?)

As noted earlier, Americans are by and large a grateful lot. Nonetheless, keeping thankfulness vibrant requires replenishment that flows from reacquaintance and renewal. To illustrate, all of us have read about or know someone who has suffered a terrible personal tragedy or illness. Periodically such news jolts us out of our complacent slumber and for a short period we recollect ourselves with thanks-filled reflections that contrast these distressful events with our own favorable situation. As creatures of habit, however, we inevitably revert back to an autopilot consciousness, exchanging our short-lived appreciations for a life of daily routine. As a consequence, awareness of blessings tapers off, and the opportunity for self-knowledge and the rediscovered recollections of fortunate conditions wither. To be sure, terrorism on American shores and the aftermath of 9/11 have shattered the misconceptions that two oceans or friendly neighbors can protect us. As such, there is a heightened sense of who we are as Americans and what we are grateful for. Similarly, the recent economic downturn leaves many struggling and more aware of what they *do* have as they cope with financial adversity. Still, in the trenches of everyday life, we adapt so well or get so caught up in the immediate situation that conscious appreciation falters. Not to belabor the point, but again consider the question: Have you given enough time in the last week to the gratitude you have for the gifts of life, family, friends, a job, or just the ability to sleep safely at night?

A taken-for-granted existence poses, perhaps, the most serious threat to the goal of living gratefully. It is not that Americans as a whole are not grateful, because, as we have seen, Americans enthusiastically endorse a sense of being blessed. Yet, I suspect that unless questioned specifically about their blessings or unless their focus is drawn expressly to the many benefits they enjoy, far too many Americans live take-it-for-granted lives and, therefore, are frequently oblivious to the gifts they enjoy.

GRATITUDE LIMITS OUR SELFISH DESIRES

Gratitude helps immunize us against unrestrained wants. A flu shot safeguards the body from the virus. Similarly (though admittedly we cannot go about quantifying gratitude), maintaining steady doses of thanksgiving partially safeguards us against consumerism's subtle lures. Our modern economy relies on a vast array of forces: the stock market, investor trading, new technologies, competition, advertising, and corporate mergers, to name just a few. However, nearly every facet of the American economy must in one way or another bow to the central role of consumer spending. The enormous purchasing power and the continued willingness of Americans (until the recent economic decline) to take on debt signal the power and reach of a consumer-oriented mentality. Glitzy ad campaigns target specific audiences. Both because of the availability of credit and because of part-time employment, teens, for example, possess enormous purchasing power (spending more than 150 billion dollars annually).[26] This select group is continuously exposed to hi-tech commercials and theme-oriented ads. To emphasize this point, I recently viewed a television news segment demonstrating how companies purposely target children (four- to eleven-year-olds). With fine-tuned advertising, these preteens become sophisticated "pre" mature consumers whose allegiance to brand names translates to urgent pleas beseeching increasingly exasperated parents!

One aspect of consumerism deserves particular attention: consumerism centering around the rapid nature of product change. Our high-tech world amply dramatizes this reality. I admit I possess scant knowledge about computer science or the merits of specific software applications, and thus I rely heavily on the advice of more knowledgeable friends. All the same, no one escapes the observation that technological change is swift and relentless. Computers are constantly altered to increase memory. Software systems require continual upgrading to provide more efficient and sophisticated applications. If we were truly honest, when it comes to personal use, it is probably true that many of these upgrades and accessories are unnecessary. The efficiency achieved, however, and the sense of power gained from the latest computer acquisition slowly yet subtly transforms the *desire* for such purchase to a sense of *need* for it. Added to this changing technology is the sheer volume of computer games and programs that compete for shelf space. Additionally, the amount of choices in supermarkets, in stores, and now on the Internet ensures that consumers, whether eight or eighty-eight, run into seemingly endless selections powered by newly acquired (and oftentimes artificially contrived) desires.

The sheer number of choices, the rapid nature of change, and the pressures to keep up and acquire more hinder and frequently undermine the capacity for gratitude. A consumer-oriented mentality focuses on, and increasingly preoccupies itself with, acquiring, replenishing, depleting, and competing. Take a moment and reflect on these four words: *acquiring, replenishing, depleting,* and *competing.* Slowly repeat these four words to yourself two or three times. What images or feelings do these four words trigger in you? I'm virtually certain that having a sense of gratitude or responding, "These four words make me feel grateful," would rarely receive a vote! The point is, of course, that over time, as the tendencies to purchase, to consume, to throw away, and to acquire more reflect our attitude and become part of daily routine, the temptation lurks that our perspectives are mentally grooved to reflect increasingly selfish ends. Such mentality ripens erroneously into a situation in which "wants" are now experienced as "needs." When taken to the extreme, this observation explains in part why children hurt, maim, or even kill one another over a pair of tennis shoes or some other insignificant item. Left unrestrained, this mind-set (aided by advertising and the illusions it generates) blossoms into a perceived reality wherein "being good" becomes equated, not with "doing something" or "being something," but with "buying something"!

In a similar vein, this worldview inevitably fashions and, with time, warps personal emotions. To emphasize this latter point, I recently viewed a television advertisement that specifically said "gratitude guaranteed." I was left with the image of a neatly wrapped package of gratitude just waiting to be delivered to my door! The notion itself is a ridiculous one. In my wildest imagination I cannot comprehend how anyone can possibly guarantee for someone else an authentic sense of gratitude through a purchase! Unfortunately, this perspective encourages in us a chronic neediness and a sense of depletion ("I need some gratitude so I better buy it"). When experienced, the only recourse to rectify such emptiness is increased purchasing. Buying something might even trigger a short-lived feeling of gratitude or the fleeting expression "thank-you" as we purchase a product, but such thankful states are short-lived as consumer consciousness veers toward the relentless drive to discard, to use up, or to acquire something better. An ironic aspect of such consumerism is the undeniable fact that over the years, as material goods and income have increased, the level of happiness has remained relatively stable. It has been shown over and over that neither accumulating money nor acquiring an ever-expanding number of possessions is likely to promote a greater sense of happiness![27]

Obviously, there is nothing wrong, at times, with spending money! Necessities must be bought. Treating ourselves with a night out, some attractive clothing or a well-deserved vacation, or even being surprised by an unexpected trip purchased by a loved one for our benefit, frequently serves to restore a sense of balance to our lives. It goes without saying that purchasing can create a sense of joy and serenity. Even more important from the perspective of gratitude, we know that buying something for someone usually expresses love and affection and so is very often an appropriate sign of a grateful heart. What must be pointed out, however, is that the temptation to adopt a consumer mentality requires continual monitoring to ensure that healthy contentment is not supplanted by corroding consumerism, breeding in the process dissatisfaction, letdowns, and endless cynicism. Living gratefully rejects consumer-oriented consciousness. Indeed, the evidence indicates that grateful people are less likely to exhibit a buy-and-spend attitude. Research suggests that "grateful individuals place less importance on material goods; they are less likely to judge their own and others' success in terms of possessions accumulated; they are less envious of others; and are more likely to share their possessions with others relative to less grateful persons."[28] It seems that grateful people relish what they already have rather than what they must have. Gratitude takes joy in the present rather than fixing its gaze on future acquisitions. Gratitude reaches out to acknowledge another in heartfelt thanks rather than calculate wealth or indulge selfish desires. Though the economic recession that gripped not only the United States but the world in the last years of this century's first decade has caused incalculable suffering for so many, it has provided an antidote to the consumerism discussed above. Many appear awakened to a newfound appreciation of what they have and found comfort in a simpler lifestyle. Only time will tell what this might do for America's gratitude quotient.

GRATITUDE MAKES US BETTER PEOPLE

A final reason for exploring gratitude rests in the stark neglect it has received from scholars and the consequences this omission has for living noble lives. It is a commonly held view that "gratitude is a highly prized human disposition. But the concept of thankfulness, until very recently, has inspired very little systematic scientific research despite its role in our individual and collective well-being."[29] Moreover, "despite its presumed value in most of the world's religions and philosophies, psychologists have largely ignored the study of gratitude."[30] More tellingly, a scan of major studies underlines the point that social scientists fail to give adequate attention to this emotion. "Psychologists rarely think much about what makes people happy. They focus on their sadness, or what makes them anxious. That is why psychology journals have published 45,000 articles in the last 30 years on depression, but only 400 on joy."[31] Studying depression, investigating the origins of anxiety, or researching the causes underlying schizophrenia or addictions is by any measure a worthy and vital pursuit. Most understandably, unraveling the enormous complexity of these disorders has the high-minded goal to develop more promising biological and psychological interventions to lessen or alleviate human suffering and misery. Yet, doesn't human functioning consist of more than illness and disorder? What gives meaning to our lives and motivates our behaviors are again and again the hopes, the dreams, and the desires intertwined with positive emotions and ideals.

A former president of the American Psychological Association, Martin Seligman, captures well this imbalance in psychological research. He noted: "How has it happened that the social sciences view the human strengths and virtues—altruism, courage, honesty, duty, joy, health, responsibility and good cheer—as derivative, defensive or downright illusions, while weakness and negative motivations—anxiety, lust, selfishness, paranoia, anger, disorder and sadness—are viewed as authentic?"[32] Seligman challenges psychology to be a "positive" force that promotes "human strengths" and "civic virtues" in order to develop a realistic conception of what a "good life" might mean.[33] Fortunately, this emphasis on life's darker side is yielding gradually to more balanced and hopeful assessments of human behavior. "Social scientists, policy-makers, and lay-people express increasing interest in the conditions, traits, and attitudes that define quality of life."[34]

A useful and essential starting point to examine quality-of-life issues surfaces when we address the question: "How should I live my life?" Such reflection affords the opportunity to take time to establish the meaning behind living a *good* life. Humans are social animals who attach to, and bond with, individuals, groups, and wider civic communities. More specifically, for any relationship to flourish, whether it resides at an interpersonal or the broader social level, it requires the presence of rules, duties, and obligations. At some point we must flesh out (and live up to) a sense of what a good relationship means; that is, determine what behaviors define being a "good" friend, spouse, parent, team member, neighbor, or citizen.

Not surprisingly, specific ideals and virtues have to one degree or another become associated with being "good" in these roles. Among them: duty, loyalty, courage, honesty, and so on, to name just a few. Positive emotions, likewise, cluster together when we reflect on the significant roles in our lives. When we think seriously about and live out our lives as good friends, good spouses, or good parents, we can't help but be flooded with emotions such as happiness, love, hope, and gratitude. Moreover, the very act of being grateful invites us to a sense of interdependence and otherness. And otherness always sparks us to be conscious of life outside ourselves. Starkly stated: there is more than the all-powerful "I"; there is more than "me." This relating and sharing builds on the very moral quality contained in relationships themselves. How we speak, what we say, and the manner in which we respond always revert back to the goodness we carry within and are motivated to carry out. In short, what we do by way of our actions speaks directly to who we *are* interiorly. More broadly, the experience of gratitude is integral to any fundamental meaning of living a good life. Gratitude serves to bond us to our most cherished loves and, more widely, as groups of citizens to more broad-based communities (neighborhoods, parishes, social clubs), even to a national identity (recall again the positive feelings that Thanksgiving Day elicits). As the preceding observations indicate, gratitude surfaces as a strong candidate, indeed, a key ingredient, for a positive psychology that champions human strengths and ideals.

A Caution

Having viewed the numerous positive features of gratitude, we need to take a step back in order to avoid falling into the trap of the Pollyannaish bias. This bias occurs when we evaluate something in a solely positive light. Given the beneficial qualities of gratitude, the temptation exists to give it a pass and dwell entirely on its positive aspects. Yet, we need to think critically about any subject and gratitude is no exception. For example, consider the emotion of love. When we think of someone we love, we normally recall many joyful moments, soothing images of contentment, and periodic experiences of bliss. Yet, are there not many types of love? Are all equally beneficial? Indeed, aren't some emotional experiences that are naively identified as love really "false" loves? Or, likewise, that an expression of love, even though well intended, is inappropriate? Or might we not erroneously construe an emotional state as love when in fact the feeling deceptively obscures an underlying, unhealthy dependency or masks an attempt on our part or someone else's to manipulate? Thus, though readily attracted to the emotion of love, we must not approach it uncritically or fail to examine its meaning both within ourselves and in the context of our relationships.

Gratitude, likewise (as we will see in chapter 4), requires scrutiny.[35] It goes without saying that people overwhelmingly and enthusiastically endorse gratitude! Yet, can we not display gratitude inappropriately? Most certainly. Are there instances where a false gratitude promotes manipulation? Absolutely. Can gratitude, when distorted, foster unethical behaviors? Unfortunately, yes! Parallel to our critical look at the emotion of love, then, the emotion of gratitude requires careful and thoughtful examination. Given its popularity and appeal, the Pollyannaish bias requires that gratitude receive close examination. Not to end on a souring note, however, in the vast majority of instances everyone benefits from gratitude! Far more often than not, the expression of gratitude is a most worthwhile and deeply cherished experience.

Discovering the Meaning of Gratitude: A First Look

Unless suffering from severe intellectual or neurological impairment, every human possesses the capacity for gratitude. Of course, being capable of gratitude is distinct from the desire to have gratitude. Likewise, a person who only occasionally feels grateful is a far cry from the individual who continually strives to cultivate a grateful heart. All this having been said, even while reading this book, the reader knows gratitude when he or she witnesses it and most certainly has felt it on numerous occasions. In the chapters ahead, we journey on a road that allows us to understand in a profound way the richness and depth of gratitude and how to incorporate it into our everyday lives profitably. At this early point in our discussion, since we are familiar with many occasions of gratitude in our lives, we only briefly sketch the features of gratitude, what we define as its basic *structure*, which forms the foundation for the gratitude experience that we probe and elaborate upon in the chapters ahead.

First, all agree that gratitude is a positive experience; it is associated with many pleasant feelings, such as awe, joy, and contentment. Second, depending on what has evoked our gratitude, we feel affirmed, more alive, and enriched by our experience. More precisely, gratitude appears to flow from our enhanced sense of well-being.

Third, the source for the good that has happened to us is the recognition that something or, more than likely, the generosity of someone has brought about the improvement in our well-being. As a consequence, we find ourselves feeling a sense of having been gifted by the good fortune or generosity shown us. Stated another way, due to another's kindness, something has been added to our life. Finally, as a result of feeling grateful, we are disposed to respond in some way. As an example, when I need some advice, I can go to my friend who, even though she is busy, carves out time to listen to my concern. I know she has my best interest in mind when offering advice. I leave our conversation feeling better about my situation. Now energized, I feel more confident and prepared to face the challenge ahead. At the same time, I look forward to the time when I can help my friend in return or respond in a similarly favorable manner to someone else in need. In other words, the *dynamic* of gratitude lies in the fact that goodness has come to us, and it is goodness we give back. Thus, at a bare minimum, we can say that when we feel grateful we are talking about (1) a positive experience in which (2) we have benefited (have felt gifted by) because (3) something has happened or someone has done something for us (gifted us) that (4) leads us, more often than not, to do something positive in kind. More succinctly, we could summarize these four points as, simply, the positive sense associated with gift given, received, and given away—or, put another way (and this gets at the essential nature of the gratitude experience), the heart of our gratitude experience is best reflected, simply, by the phrase *the giving away of goodness*.

In sum, the four features mentioned above make up what is more or less the structure of gratitude.[36] The actual receiving, accepting, and responding to the gift is the dynamic of gratitude. As we explore gratitude in the chapters ahead, we will frequently see examples of both its structure and its dynamic.

A Final Comment

The ideas and themes that emerge in the pages ahead are the product of several sources. Obviously, my own study, reflections, and thoughts form the basis for exploring the nature and effects of gratitude. This basis has benefited from a number of resources. Several colleagues and friends have shared their own ideas and pointed me in directions I otherwise would have neglected or ignored. In addition, I have profited from conversations with a large number of individuals who shared their own thoughts on gratitude. These discussions were wide ranging and informative. Initially, I asked the simple questions: "What do you mean by gratitude?" and "Could you describe some experience in which you felt grateful?" In a remarkably short time, several themes emerged that provided a catalyst for further questions added to subsequent interviews. In addition, several surveys about the meaning of gratitude were conducted with young, middle, and older adults. To highlight the meaning of gratitude, I also included interviews or questionnaires from individuals who had recently completed either a week- or month-long retreat. In the pages ahead I describe, when helpful, others' remarks and periodically quote specific, personal statements or stories. In this way, gratitude truly comes alive as the human experience it is. Thus, the thoughts offered in these pages are the product not only of the author; they are also the fruitful reflections of people who experience gratitude in their daily lives.

The Daily Gratitude Inventory (DGI)

In the chapters ahead we will offer a variety of strategies, questions, and exercises to promote gratitude. For now, a useful starting point is just increasing our consciousness of how *blessed* we are and, in the process, how grateful we can easily be if we put our minds to it. We have already put forth the theme that life is a continual invitation to gratitude. If this is true, then we must seek to discover these invitations in the ups and downs of daily life. As noted above, we all too frequently take for granted so many of our blessings. One effective way to sensitize ourselves to the numerous benefits experienced and blessings received is to employ what spiritual writers describe as a daily examen. A generation or two ago this might have been called an examination of conscience. Examining our conscience entails developing the habit of selecting a short period of time on a daily basis in order to review our day, acknowledging our failings and faults and then resolving to do better in the days that follow. Examining conscience on a daily basis has a number of goals. It sensitizes us to our weaknesses, fosters awareness of the moral standards we wish to uphold (by recollecting our faults and missteps), attempts to foster a sense of personal forgiveness, and seeks to motivate us to live upright lives in the future.

Strictly speaking, whereas the purpose of an examination of conscience is to promote sorrow for wrongdoing and subsequent changes in behavior, the purpose of a daily examen is to expand *consciousness* around some theme or area of our lives that we wish to improve. In this case, what we are attempting to expand is a grateful heart through greater awareness of blessings. In short, the Daily Gratitude Inventory (DGI) is, in essence, a daily examen for gratitude. Daily use of the DGI raises our consciousness of blessings received and instills a gratefulness that spills out in our attitudes and behaviors. Continuing use of the DGI will make us more sensitive to the goodness that is both within and around us. Some readers familiar with the thinking of St. Ignatius will see his influence in the DGI below. Many centuries ago Ignatius developed an examen that allowed for a daily probing of God's working in one's life. In addition, he constantly championed the need for gratitude and rarely failed to take the opportunity to encourage gratitude in his brother Jesuits and those he worked with. Advocating gratitude became one of his life goals (one in which he admirably succeeded, as we shall see in the next chapter). With all the above in mind, I have little doubt that he would be fully behind a twenty-first-century Jesuit psychologist's attempt to develop an examen whose purpose was to increase the living of life gratefully!

The DGI is divided into four parts:

1. Pausing. The first requirement of the DGI is to find a daily time to practice it. Most people choose the evening, because, as their day draws to a close, they find themselves in a reflective mood. But the important point is to find a time that fits your schedule. Accordingly, early morning, a break at midday, late at night, or any other time might prove profitable. Many people experiment until they find a suitable time that is most convenient. When you do find the time that is best, spend a few moments in quiet. Settle yourself and breathe deeply in and out until you find yourself in a relaxed state.

2. Reviewing. As you relax, begin to recall your day. Here it is helpful to break down the day's events into several categories and to reflect on what has "happened" in the previous twenty-four hours. Three categories that might prove helpful are the following:

The Everyday:
The scent of the air or a fragrance that caught my fancy...
The taste of a drink or the texture of a certain food...
The colors of nature or a specific scene that attracted me...
The recognition of an idea I had or putting to good use some
   creative energy...

Significant People:
Someone who gave me some time or went out of his or her
   way for me...
A person who offered me guidance and counsel...
A person I love and have deep affection for...
A friend who...

My Life:
A strength or talent (e.g., health, intelligence, a personal
   trait)...
A feeling I felt this day...
An insight that came to me this day...
An experience that helped me to grow...

The above is just one example of what your DGI might look like. Construct various categories and themes that appeal to you and prompt your sense for feeling grateful. One important point to make is that *quality* is more important than quantity! In other words, *as you go through your day, be attentive to the fact that gratitude-in-depth is more important than gratitude-by-the-numbers*. Accordingly, as you review your day and you find yourself moved toward one or two instances in particular—for example, the kindness of a friend or happiness over an insight you had—stick with them. There is no need to try to go through an entire inventory of events. Be attentive above all to the *quality* of the gratitude experience you are having.

3. Relishing. After reflecting for a few moments on the reasons for your gratitude and its effects throughout this day, make a conscious effort to shift your focus by repeating several times the word *gift*. Slowly repeat the word, or a similar phrase such as "I am gifted," or "I have been gifted," several times. Now link the word *gift* with each person, event, or experience that you previously recollected and that has inspired your gratitude today. Begin to view all of these encounters and experiences that have prompted your gratitude over the past few moments to be "gifts" you have been given or have received over a twenty-four-hour period. Take some time to savor the notion that you have been gifted. Engage your imagination as a person with these many gifts. Recast your life as a gift. What is it like to be so gifted? Spend time recalling the many gifts you have been given since the last time you made your DGI.

4. Responding. The final part of the DGI begins with a question: *Now that I have sensed myself as having been gifted, in what ways can I give back for the many ways I have been gifted today?* Resolve not to keep your gifts to yourself! What are some creative ways you might share your gifts with others? True gratitude occurs when a gift-receiver becomes a gift-giver. Consider ways that you can give back to others for the many gifts you have been given. Your gift-giving should reflect who you are—your life history, your strengths, your situation—and what you feel moved to do. Some responses to being gifted might include:

Lessening a specific behavior
Increasing a specific behavior
Reaching out to someone
Trying something new
Attempting to modify an attitude
Offering support, whether financial or emotional
Giving someone some time
Surprising someone
Volunteering for something
Donating something
Considering a point of view other than your own

In sum, the DGI consists of pausing, reviewing, relishing, and responding: I attend to my gratitude, I look for it in my life, I savor it, and I give back to others.

We began this chapter with a broad overview of gratitude and explored its significance for twenty-first-century living. We conclude the chapter by offering a sense of what gratitude is and suggesting ways to increase the gratitude experience in daily life. We are now ready to embark on a fuller exploration of this vital human emotion and to discover ways to live more authentically and fully a grateful heart.

Chapter Two

GRATEFUL REASONING

The grateful acknowledgment of blessings received is loved and
esteemed not only on earth but in heaven.

—St. Ignatius Loyola

When examined closely, gratitude appears both rich and complex.
Derived from the Latin *gratia*, *gratitude* means "grace," "graciousness,"
or "gratefulness." In all of the world's major religions—Judaism,
Christianity, Islam, Buddhism, and Hinduism—gratitude is a highly
valued disposition that believers are encouraged to cultivate by daily
practice. "Indeed, the consensus among the world's religious and ethical writers is that people are obligated to feel and express gratitude
in response to received benefits."[1] Major religious traditions incorporate a sense of gratitude in worship and prayer, and gratitude to God
is an essential and common theme urged on believers. As an emotion, gratitude, next to love, is likely the most common emotion
desired among the faithful, considering that a grateful sense connects
us not only to God but to our neighbor as well.[2] This is readily apparent in the Christian tradition, for worship of God, the primary object
of our gratitude, is best expressed and lived out through the gratitude
we have for our brothers and sisters in community. It is surely not an
exaggeration to note that "for many people, gratitude is at the core
of spiritual and religious experience."[3] Moreover, the word *thanks* and
closely related words such as *thankful*, *thankfulness*, and *thanksgiving*
appear more than 150 times in the Bible (both Old and New
Testaments). The best descriptions of the central place of gratitude
in the Christian life are found in the writings of the apostle Paul. Of
the seventy New Testament expressions of thanksgiving, the majority appear in the epistles of the Pauline tradition.[4] Letters written to
various Christian communities commonly begin with some reference
of gratitude, and frequently he exhorts Christians to respond both to

27

the Lord and to one another with thanks. For Paul, a grateful sense is linked to the graces the Lord offers us. Indeed, Paul makes numerous references to grace in his writing, and the New Testament Greek word for grace, *charis*, means gift.[5]

St. Ignatius: Saint of Gratitude

Although a number of Christian saints, such as Thomas Aquinas and Bernard of Clairvaux, wrote about the virtues of gratitude, it is Ignatius Loyola who made gratitude the core of his approach to God. Ignatius did not leave us with any learned treatise or systematic treatment of gratitude. The centrality that gratitude had for Ignatius is culled through an examination of his letters (Ignatius was an avid letter writer), his *Spiritual Diary*, the *Constitutions of the Society of Jesus*, and the *Spiritual Exercises*. Pulling together all these sources, the Jesuit spiritual theologian Gerald Fagin has provided a masterful treatment of the role and significance of gratitude in Ignatius's life.[6]

A member of Spanish nobility, Ignatius was born at Loyola in 1491. As was common for men of his age and social position, he received a military education and became a soldier. Caught up in the social upheaval that so marked early sixteenth-century Europe, he was wounded in the leg by a cannonball as he led the defense of his homeland at the siege of Pamplona in 1521. During his recuperation at the family home, the only books available to him were two spiritual volumes. His reading of these books and the subsequent contemplation it engendered altered his life forever. Rejecting his previous way of life, he dedicated himself to a life of prayer and service to God.

After his conversion, Ignatius embarked upon a journey to follow the Lord wherever it might lead. His spiritual journey led him to experience numerous graced encounters, including mystical communication and the forming of a band of companions that eventually became known as the Society of Jesus (Jesuits). Throughout his spiritual journey, Ignatius paid particular attention to his own interior movements. One of the fruits of this interior scrutiny was his composing of the meditations and insights he had experienced, which became known in book form as the *Spiritual Exercises* and which has significantly influenced both spiritual thinking and formation over the centuries. This volume, divided into four parts (each termed a "week"), has served as the basis for retreats for countless individuals for over four hundred years. "It is not a book *on* spirituality; it is, rather, a book *of* spirituality."[7] As such, reading the book is secondary to *doing* it, taking it to heart, and practicing it in everyday life. Combining prayer, meditations, contemplation, and self-examination when making the *Spiritual Exercises*, the retreatants are led to discern more sensitively where God is leading them while strengthening them in making decisions that more clearly reflect the Lord's will. The goal of the retreat based on the *Spiritual Exercises* is a deepening interior freedom to follow the Lord's call, which leads to loving service in the building of God's kingdom.

The spiritual theologian Wilkie Au recently observed that the *Spiritual Exercises* lead one to what he terms "Ignatian service," which is characterized by appreciating, living in, and calling the world to a transformation modeled on the Lord's own life of discipleship.[8] Au correctly notes that the *Spiritual Exercises* are not something we analyze and dissect; rather, they are to be lived out in how we love and the gratitude we have. He goes on to show how gratitude is the energizing theme that pervades each step of the retreatant's journey. A short treatment of Au's essential points follows:

First, the *Spiritual Exercises* begin with the meditation First Principle and Foundation, which emphasizes that everything is created by a God who loves us and provides us with everything we could possibly need. As a consequence, our principal response in this first meditation becomes one of gratitude.

Second, during the first week of the *Exercises*, we are confronted with our sinfulness, yet we realize that though we are sinful, God's loving embrace stirs us to respond gratefully.

Third, in the transition between the first and second weeks, Ignatius invites us to meditate on the Call of the King. We come to know Jesus as calling us to partner with him in loving service. We are grateful that, though sinners, we too are called to carry on Jesus' message.

Fourth, the second week of the *Exercises* finds us grateful for the life of Jesus, who incarnates God's compassionate and unconditional love for his creatures. Again, our response for the gift of Jesus can only be gratitude.

Fifth, with the third week of the *Exercises,* we are drawn to reflect on and contemplate how strong God's love for us truly is, for we realize in gratitude that God, out of love, not only became one of us, but also died an ignoble death.

Sixth, in the fourth week, we meet the transforming yet consoling power of Jesus' resurrection. We find ourselves grateful for the limitless offering of grace that Jesus' triumph over death now creates. In gratitude, we come to the ever-deepening realization that our life-perspective is altered irrevocably by Jesus' redemptive act. Because Jesus has triumphed, so too we as his brothers and sisters have triumphed, a victory for which we are grateful and which calls us to loving service in the kingdom.

And lastly, in the final prayer experience—the Contemplation to Attain Love—we come gratefully to understand more than ever before that our lives are gifts from a loving God and that the only possible response we can give to a God who loves us so totally is grateful service.[9]

As a most fitting end to the *Spiritual Exercises,* the Contemplation to Attain Love highlights the theme of gratitude in a markedly profound way. Ignatius begins with the two famous sayings about love being shown in deeds rather than words, and about love consisting in mutual interchange, in the sharing of goods, in what we might call gift-giving. Already here, gratitude is an implicit theme. The mutual gift-giving expresses a foundational role for gratitude in our relationship with God. Moreover, this gratitude leads us to desire more and more to be drawn into God's loving embrace, a desire expressed most eloquently in the prayer Take, Lord, Receive. The generative force that draws this love forward is gratitude. Gradually, this gratitude embeds itself ever more naturally and effortlessly in our personalities. We move from simply responding to God with "thank-you" to a sense of God's gracious presence in all things.

Since by training I am a psychologist rather than a spiritual theologian, I refer the reader to both Fagin's and Au's fine treatments of Ignatius and gratitude for a thorough understanding of its role in Ignatius's life and thought. Still, three observations are in order:

1. Ignatius, more than any spiritual writer I know, lived and breathed gratitude. I am not suggesting he was the most grateful saint or writer in Christianity's history! Quite frankly, neither I nor anyone else can answer this question with certainty, but we could argue persuasively that he was "right up there." What we *can* conclude is that no figure in Christianity, perhaps except for Paul, understood the central importance of gratitude for becoming Christ-like and living Christian holiness. Nothing more illustrates the immensity (and intensity) of Ignatius's gratitude than his gift of tears. At times he was so engulfed in tears that praying or presiding at Mass became nearly impossible. Indeed, tearing up so interfered with his praying the Office and caused his eyes such harm that other Jesuits sought for him a papal dispensation. With his tears he experienced profound spiritual consolation and joy, stirred no doubt by his gratitude for graces received.[10] Reading Ignatius's words over the years, I would readily assert that he was overwhelmed with gratitude. For Ignatius, gratitude was a response of freedom to the many gifts bestowed on us by a loving Creator, and our grateful response must always be the proper use of our gifts to further, as a brother or sister in discipleship, Jesus' saving message. Gratitude occupied such a pivotal role in Ignatius's experience that we could describe him as having gratitude "in his blood." It was, so to speak, both his spiritual and emotional life-source: his touchstone for remembering that God had graced him, and the lens he faithfully used to view and understand his world.

2. Ignatius always made reference to experience. Anyone making the *Spiritual Exercises* is moved to the realization that God's loving touch continually reaches us through the concrete reality of daily life. What we experience is a world lovingly created by God, and as we immerse ourselves in the reality that surrounds us, the more we come to know the loving God who created us, has given us everything, and calls us to himself. This realization takes place both externally as we engage our world and internally as we acquire greater self-insight. To know and encounter the world is to know and love God who created it. Our entire life history, likewise, is actually our response to the beckoning of God to us through his Son, Jesus, who calls us to discipleship and service, and who enlists us, by decisions and choices born of gratitude, to follow his path as a transforming source for love in this world. Our grace-filled experiences of Jesus become our way to know God. These experiences include prayer and Eucharist and call us to a distinctive way of life as his followers.

3. *Ignatius was an optimist.* His optimism is rooted in God's love, which is always stronger than both the selfish inclinations we find within ourselves and the obstacles and evil we confront in our daily lives and the world as a whole. Evil does exist, for humans do thwart, twist, and misuse the freedom we are given. But we are created in God's image, and God desires that we use our freedom in partnership with him to build his Son's kingdom. Our goal is always greater interior freedom, which sheds us of our selfishness so that we are increasingly disposed to be who God desires us to be. As such, we embrace the world with service to it, always trying to find more and better ways to be a graced presence in it. Finally, when the above happens, our optimism becomes infectious. We are of service together, each building the other up through the relationships forged in the community of the church, where the memory of Jesus remains most alive and which nurtures the daily communities in which we find ourselves, such as friendships, family, school, work, and so on.

Given all that is said above, it seems that gratitude can only be acquired when we honestly engage ourselves and practice serious self-examination. Decision making and service, both so key in Ignatius's vision, only find their true authenticity when they arise from the freedom that comes from knowing who we are and why we do what we do. When this self-knowledge combines with gratitude, we are most apt to be conscious of and present to God's loving touch and to respond with the heartfelt desire for selfless service. As a consequence, it requires ongoing effort to gain insight into how God has worked and is working through us. In order to do this, we must constantly employ some form of *grateful reasoning*. Grateful reasoning might best be defined as *mindful reflection on our commitments in order to discover the depth of our gratitude*. In other words, who we are is best reflected through the commitments we have chosen, and the more we are aware of the benefits that flow from them, the more we elicit the gratitude that stirs us to engage the world and serve it selflessly. Our deepest commitments capture our hearts in ways that no other interests can. Our affection for them might know no bounds. I proffer the point that it is inconceivable to be without them; and indeed, we may well shudder when even considering their absence from our lives. Along with prayer, grateful reasoning about such commitments is the quality that most leads us to embrace Ignatius's vision. That is, being mindful as Christians of our ongoing commitments leads us to recollect how we have cooperated with God's grace, while reminding us of his graced presence in our lives now and suggesting where our graced responding might lead in the future.

An Experience of Grateful Reasoning

Several years ago I celebrated my twenty-fifth anniversary as a Jesuit priest. Like many others who achieve such a milestone, this event led me fondly to recall numerous instances of gratitude over the previous quarter-century. One event in particular had proven pivotal for my vocation. I would like to share this experience as a way to introduce the close association between gratitude and commitment and to develop from it a format that allows you to explore the gratitude you feel for the commitments in your own life journey.

A few years before my silver jubilee, I had taken part along with a group of other middle-aged Jesuits in the final stage of Jesuit training, which is commonly referred to in Jesuit circles as *tertianship*. Ignatius envisioned the tertianship as an opportunity for a Jesuit to step back from his ministry in order to redirect both his energy and his focus to his spiritual life and where God is leading him. From another vantage point, having taken first vows (upon the successful completion of the novitiate, a man's first two years as a Jesuit), completed the long course of studies that (for most Jesuits) leads to ordination, and engaged in a number of years of priestly work (which might consist in research and teaching, parish work, spiritual ministries, or many other ministerial pursuits too numerous to list), a Jesuit is wisely instructed by Ignatius to commit to a period of time where he can discover anew and, to the degree necessary, nurture and rekindle the fervor that first attracted and led him to seek entrance into the Society of Jesus. Stated another way, tertianship is a time for a middle-aged Jesuit, seasoned by his own life experience in ministry, to use a time-out period (which tertianship provides) to reacquaint himself and fall in love with God in a whole new way. When I finished describing in an elaborate fashion the tertianship experience for which I was preparing, a lay friend of mine said simply, "Sounds to me, Charlie, like a spiritual sabbatical." Upon reflection, my friend's pithy description was a much better summary than my own long-winded explanation!

On a practical note, a variety of options is available to a Jesuit as he prepares for tertianship. He can take part in a whole-year program. Some Jesuits choose to go overseas and have as part of their tertianship a third-world experience. Others might opt for a semester away from their current ministry with an additional summer tacked on. For a variety of reasons, a Jesuit might also choose a two-summer experience. I chose this latter option because of the need to maintain my psychotherapy practice (I couldn't afford to be absent from clients for a nine- or twelve-month stretch). My two-summer tertianship took me to a Jesuit community on the West Coast where I joined eleven other Jesuits; we dozen priests became tertian brothers and, consequently, the "tertian class" for this two-summer program. Besides the dozen tertians, there were two older Jesuits who were codirectors of the program.

Though the day-to-day formats of the various tertianships vary, several elements are common to each no matter what time frame the Jesuit chooses. Usually, for Americans, since Jesuits come together for tertianship from all over the United States and frequently there are a few non-American Jesuits making the tertianship as well (one of my tertian brothers was from Asia and another from Australia), they do not know personally or at least do not know well many of the men who make up their tertian class. Consequently, during tertianship they spend time socializing, swapping ministry stories, and organizing structured time to share their life histories with one another. From these many encounters, there frequently develops a trust and bond among the tertians, and many a time close friendships are formed between some men. Another common feature of tertianship is the time designated to studying documents of the Society of Jesus, such as its laws (the *Constitutions*) and other relevant writings produced by the Society (such as important letters from Father General).

By far the most significant experience, and the linchpin that holds the tertianship together, is the month set aside for the tertians to be directed in the *Spiritual Exercises*. A Jesuit first encounters the *Spiritual Exercises* during his two-year novitiate. Through his years as a Jesuit, every man sets aside annually eight days to make a retreat often based on a shortened version of the *Exercises*. With tertianship, the Jesuit once again completes the full *Exercises*.

What are the results of tertianship? After its completion, most Jesuits feel a deepened commitment to their vocation and a renewed vigor to serve the Lord and his church. Many men return to their current apostolic ministry with a deepened or newly discovered zeal. At times, the fruits of tertianship lead a Jesuit, in dialogue with his superiors, to test out or embark upon a new ministry where he can serve, in companionship with his brothers, the people of God. For all Jesuits, a most critical consequence of tertianship is the willingness to be called to final vows by the Society. With final vows, a Jesuit achieves full incorporation in the Society. To paraphrase one older Jesuit, final vows are like a married couple reaching a milestone together (such as a silver or golden anniversary). Each of the spouses knows the other's strengths and weaknesses, positive virtues and human foibles, and knowing all this they reaffirm and celebrate once again their "yes" to each other. Following a similar pattern, after all these years the Society of Jesus and the individual Jesuit know each other well and wish, through final vows, to formally cement their relationship.

Needless to say, upon completing the *Spiritual Exercises* (affectionately known among Jesuits as the Long Retreat), tertians almost invariably find themselves deeply grateful for the experience as well as for their Jesuit vocation. The month-long retreat enables a Jesuit better to realize and appreciate the Lord's mysterious workings in his life, and the meditations and prayer each tertian utilizes during the retreat are a source of surprise and insight into God's loving care for him over these many years.

After completing the retreat, my tertian brothers and I spent several days discussing among ourselves the fruits of the Long Retreat. Psychologically this made sense, for our discussion helped us to debrief each other and reinforced in each of us the graced experience we had undergone over this thirty-day period. Furthermore, the opportunity to spend time together talking over the effects of our Long Retreat experience very much coincided with Ignatius's own desire for Jesuits. Ignatius insisted that Jesuits engage in spiritual conversation as a way to encourage awareness of graces received, and this conversation did just that. Our animated discussion was both free and wide ranging. Shortly into our conversation it dawned on me that the central theme we were speaking about was, simply, gratitude. More precisely, our conversation together was actually a discussion of the reasons we were grateful for being Jesuits. Making this retreat helped each of us to realize how grateful we were that we (a) had entered the Society, (b) had remained faithful through good times and in bad to our Jesuit commitment, and (c) had made tertianship and looked forward to final vows. I felt that the richness of our conversation should not be limited just to our small group but, rather, deserved and most assuredly would benefit a wider audience. In other words, the thoughts we shared spoke a lot about the blessings derived from any life commitment—not just that of being a Jesuit—and the inherent gratitude we feel when we listen and respond to God's call to live out our commitments faithfully. Accordingly, I began to take notes on our conversation and transcribed the reasons we tertians felt grateful. My tertian brothers, seeing the worthwhile nature of the project, graciously granted me permission to commit our words to paper. For me, now several years removed from this conversation, writing down these reasons made eminent sense. I truly feel that what transpired over those few days was a powerfully expressive, graced conversation. Quite frankly, to this day it remains the most significant graced conversation I have ever participated in as a group member. To document it only made sense because such goodness needed to be shared with a wider audience and, to paraphrase the thought of Ignatius, grace is something we share, not keep to ourselves.

What follows below are the twelve "grateful reasons" for remaining Jesuits that surfaced during these several days of graced conversation. Each of the reasons is first listed separately, and following each one is a brief summary of the tertian discussion that expresses the listed grateful theme. In order to capture the personal nature of the discussion and allow the reader to enter more fully into the group discussion, I use the first person in the short description that follows each reason for gratitude. These brief explanations accurately reflect and summarize the ideas expressed by the tertians and in some instances are nearly identical to what was actually said during the meeting. It is my hope, of course, that the reader will find the grateful reasons presented below as inspirational. By this I don't mean that our tertian class consisted of a bunch of saints! We were (and are) as flawed as anyone! By inspiring I simply mean that what this conversation demonstrated very concretely is that the Lord truly, as Ignatius notes, beckons us to unite with him and that he uses us in ways that dispose us to celebrate his goodness and to build his kingdom. When we think about it, any time we cooperate in allowing the Lord to use us is justification for deeply heartfelt celebration!

To help readers appreciate the reasons as well as apply them to their lives, I offer at the end of each grateful reason several reflection questions.

Naturally, most of the readers of these pages are not Jesuits, so reading why Jesuits are grateful for their Jesuit vocations and desire to remain Jesuits, though hopefully inspiring, still leaves the question: How is this helpful for me in my life and for what I do? A fair question, to say the least! The reasons given below, though arguably specific to a Jesuit and his vocation, are in reality a springboard for understanding any life commitment. Briefly, we are most apt to be faithful to, abide by, and live out any commitment—whether it be to a spouse through marriage, another person in our life history through friendship, a type of work through our job or career, or a life choice, whether it be marriage, the single life, or a religious vocation—when we feel a grateful heart toward this commitment. Thus, these Jesuits' reasons for gratitude for their Jesuit vocation will be followed by a format that allows readers to use the reasons to generate gratitude for their own commitments.

A Conversation about Jesuit Gratitude

Below are twelve reasons why Jesuits are grateful for their vocations (commitment to the Society of Jesus). Each reason is followed by a brief personal summary of the reason and by several questions to allow the reader to personalize the reason within the context of his or her own life.

1. The Society of Jesus helps me to live my life as a healthy adult.

As I reflect upon my years in the Society, I have a deepening sense of what it means to experience healthy adulthood. The Society is an integral force in my evolving sense of myself as whole, complex, and healthy. The kindness of some superiors, the insights of several spiritual directors, the ministry opportunities offered me, and the enduring and enriching friendships that have transpired over the years—all have been occasions for substantive growth in my life. Moreover, the Society is the best place I know to be challenged and to mature. As a Jesuit, in the years ahead I will continue to succeed and fail, to feel joy and know sorrow, to apprehend my goodness and confront my darkness. All of the foregoing experiences and encounters will occasion in me a greater freedom and more honest choosing in the ways I follow Jesus.

For the reader:

- Which choices in my life have most enabled me to become a healthier adult? Spend a few moments identifying them.
- Which commitments (relationships and activities in my life) most promote in me a healthy sense of maturity?
- Which commitments have impeded a healthy sense of maturity?

2. The Society of Jesus truly does make a difference in this world and I am proud to be part of it.

I joined the Society to "make a difference," and one of the things I am most proud of is that the Jesuits truly do have this type of impact. As Matthew's Gospel reminds us (Matt 5:13–16), we are called through our actions to be a "salt" for this world and a "light" to others. The Society of Jesus offers me a place where I am this salt and light. Flipping through one of the annual yearbooks of the Society, I can't help but feel pride and excitement about the innumerable and creative ways it brings the Gospel to men and women around the globe through sustained and often imaginative apostolic undertakings. Much of this impact is due to the organizational and systematic reach of the Society through its institutions, such as retreat houses, parishes, specialized ministerial associations, and a well-established educational system. These endeavors challenge me to be my best. Yet, there are also always Jesuits who as individuals discover original and innovative apostolic undertakings. They establish an institute, organize a boycott, engage the arts, fashion an idea, or simply take their ardor and imagination and go off and initiate, do, or reinvigorate something that bears fruit. I am proud of my small contribution to this overall effect, but what has changed for me is that I feel part of all these other efforts, too. We really are all in this together.

For the reader:

- As I examine the significant choices I have made over the years, which have made the most difference for those I most love and care for?
- Given who I am at this moment in my life, are there some decisions I can make, either now or in the near future, that would allow me to make creatively a greater contribution to the Gospel and to others' lives? What might these be? What must I do, alter, or adjust in my life to bring about this creativity?

3. My time in the Society has increased my own sense of meaning and purpose.

Over the years, the documents of recent congregations have helped me to develop a viewpoint for engaging the world. For me, this perspective most resides in the Society's insistence that our apostolic ventures be utilized for serving faith and promoting justice. Reviewing my years in the Order, I have come more and more to find that the ideas championed by the Society allow me to find coherence for my life and, thus, a purpose for why I do what I do. Increasingly, there is a deeply intentional aspect to my feelings, thoughts, and behavior; in other words, a self-consistency has overtaken me that helps me solidify and respond more purposefully to people and events I encounter in my ministry. Moreover, I discover more frequently that themes emphasized by the Society play a pivotal role in how I understand, perceive, and contribute to the world with which I am engaged.

For the reader:

- As I review my life, what relationships and other commitments have proven most meaningful and given me the most sense of purpose?
- What is going on in my life right now that provides me with the most meaning and purpose?

4. It is "fun" being a Jesuit.

For me, the part of being a Jesuit that I find most enjoyable is the laughter. I like living with people with whom I can laugh. To share this merriment eases my load. It makes more bearable the pain and sorrow that come from empathizing with some of the people I encounter in my ministry. The gentle banter, playful teasing, and good laughs help keep me human and grounded. Stated most directly, over the years I have learned that the Society is a place where I should take my work seriously, but not myself too seriously. My experience has taught me that when a brother Jesuit and I succumb to the habit of taking ourselves too seriously and we disagree over an issue, then we have potentially set in place the perfect ingredients for misunderstandings. Most certainly, men who enter the Society today should be capable of genuine laughter, which includes being able to laugh at themselves.

For the reader:

- Recall decisions and choices in my life that have been the sources for joy and merriment. Take a moment and savor them.
- Reflect on the statement, "I should take my commitments seriously, but not myself too seriously." Evaluate my significant commitments by this statement. What situations lead me to take myself too seriously?

5. The Society helps me love the church.

The Society of Jesus is the best place for me to show my affection for the church. As a Jesuit I have grown in the ability to love and relate to the church in an adult way. By "adult way" I mean neither slavish obedience nor knee-jerk criticism, but rather a freely given commitment to the church with an awareness, at times, perhaps of my own ambivalence, which I both tolerate and accept. A Jesuit's life involves loving the church in part through constructive criticism that is voiced only after prayerful discernment and that always maintains the solidarity we owe the church and from which we can never be apart or separated if our work be truly Jesuit.

For the reader:

- How would I describe my commitment to my faith community or religious tradition?

- How do I live my faith commitment to my religious tradition in an *adult-like* manner?

6. *My experience of God has been deepened by being a Jesuit.*

Over my years in the Society, I have experienced God in a profound and intimate way. I can speak about it, yet there exists a degree to which the experience is enduringly elusive. The desire to share this God-experience is only natural and I have done this through teaching, homilies, and other pastoral works. Still, human explanation inevitably depicts my relationship with God in a tidy, neat package that, in the long run, proves inadequate and unhelpful. The bottom line is that my time as a Jesuit has allowed me to know God through the life, death, and resurrection of Jesus. In the Fifteenth Annotation to the *Spiritual Exercises*, Ignatius notes that God acts directly through intimate communication with his creatures, and I, as a Jesuit, have been the recipient of this amazingly gracious gesture. And the ministries in which I have participated as a Jesuit have allowed me to share this wonder with others. As I continue my life's journey in the Society, I have come more and more to believe that what constitutes me is God's love acting through me. With greater clarity I can understand the words of the Psalmist: "For you formed my inward parts, you covered me in my mother's womb. I will praise you for I am fearfully and wonderfully made" (Ps 139:13–14). My life as a Jesuit situates me so I can bask in this love, and the ministries I perform as a Jesuit provide the opportunity to share this love.

For the reader:

- Which choices and decisions in my life have provided the best opportunities for me to know the Lord?
- How has my journey toward God changed or deepened over the years? Which commitments in my life have most enhanced my experience of God?

7. *As a Jesuit, I have experienced God's faithfulness.*

As I look back on my years in the Society, or for that matter as I look back on my entire life, one certain fact stands out over and over again: the Lord's constant and continual fidelity. In retrospect, God has not let me down. No matter the high or low I am experiencing, when I gain perspective I realize that God has always watched over me, though in some instances, this insight eluded me at the actual moment. At times, my vocation has been a test of *my* faithfulness to God's faithfulness, to the Lord's always-generous love. What I continually find amazing is that God has always been there, even if I stumbled, or was too stubborn or too self-absorbed to see his handiwork. In one sense, a significant part of my vocation has been what I can at best, yet feebly, characterize as a theology of surprise! I entered the Society thinking I might be drawn to this ministry but soon found other opportunities, and then others. Superiors and Jesuit friends, likewise, surprised me through their challenges, invitations, and insights. I can truthfully say that if I have patience, take the long view, and pray for the grace, then God has a way of making the unpromising bear fruit, of transforming the painful moments into redemptive ones, and even of transforming the ho-hum events into sources of wisdom.

For the reader:

- Which choices and decisions have most led me to trust the Lord more?
- What people and situations make it most easy for me to trust? What events in my life history make it more difficult to trust the Lord on the journey he wishes for me?

8. The Society is a wonderful organization that has afforded me opportunities to learn to love freely and deeply.

The bottom line for considering any vocation is best summed up in the question: "In what state of life can I love the most?" For me, this love is made most real and comes most alive as a Jesuit. Furthermore, this love is multidimensional. It is God's unfailing love for me, my own personal relationship with the Lord, and my own desire to return his love through my work in the Society's ministries. In sum, my love is grounded in the Lord, nourished through Jesuit companionship, and shared with those to whom I minister. The late father general of the Society, Pedro Arrupe, in a statement commonly attributed to him in Jesuit lore (though never recorded), got it right when he said:

Nothing is more practical than finding God; that is, falling in love in a quite absolute, final way. What you are in love with, what seizes your imagination, will affect everything. It will decide why you get out of bed in the morning, what you will do with your evenings, how you will spend your weekends, what you read, who you know, what breaks your heart, and what amazes you with joy and gratitude. Fall in love. Stay in love. And it will decide everything.

My own spin on this statement is that I have grown in my capacity for loving unselfishly. True, I will never completely be rid of my selfish desires. Yet, I know I detect a growing generosity that demonstrates my maturing attitude and approach to life. This growth is a source of expanding contentment and fulfillment within me. The Contemplation to Attain Love is always a goal to strive for. It is anything but static. It is a forceful dynamism that I reflect simply by who I am.

For the reader:

- Which commitments in my life have made it most easy for me to love as I desire?
- Which choices or decisions in my life have hindered or impeded my desire to love others or do the most loving thing?

9. *The Society of Jesus remains for me the best place to live a life of integrity.*

When all is said and done, life continually intersects with, and is inextricably tied to, integrity. In my early years as a Jesuit I used to think of the vows as rules that needed to be followed. Over the past few decades, this thought has shifted to the vows being tied, not to rules, but rather to the definition of who I am. More and more the vows are incorporated into how I define myself. In other words, in my time in the Society, the vows are not so much rules to follow as, rather, qualities I possess. Out of this deepening of the vows flows the realization of the guiding moral principles that direct my life. As I gain this increasing moral clarity, I find myself energized, clearer regarding the path I take and the decisions I uphold. Another way to say it is that I find myself more and more standing for something. My vowed life as a Jesuit has pushed me to reflect on and think through the principles that constitute my moral core and without which I feel incomplete, if not empty.

For the reader:

- What moral principles do I use to guide my life, and to what degree do I live out these principles in each of my significant life commitments?
- How would I describe to a close friend my sense of "integrity"?

10. I have come to value Jesuit spirituality more deeply.

I have discovered that a synchrony exists between my sense of self and Jesuit spirituality. My life is one of service, and the spirituality I have embraced is one that unearths God's goodness. Jesuit spirituality continuously affirms God's incarnate presence in this world, and the Lord uses me both to uncover and to proclaim this truth. I used to think the life of a Jesuit was to create goodness in the world, but the longer I am a Jesuit the more I understand that my life is not to create goodness: it's not necessary, for goodness already exists both in me and in the world. God uses me to discover it! Moreover, by understanding Jesuit spirituality more deeply, I have come to realize my own goodness and the goodness of the world. The first step in this understanding consists in letting God love me rather than my returning love to God. The *priority* first and foremost must be letting God love me *as I am*. As I continue to embrace my commitment to Jesuit life, this transforming relationship with God leads me to the insight that because this world is good and blessed by God, I can continually strive to give away and spend myself so that my vocation is lived, ultimately, as the *gift* of goodness to others.

For the reader:

- How would I describe my spirituality to someone important to me? Which life-commitments have most shaped my spirituality? Why do I say these rather than others?
- How comfortable am I with just letting God love me as I am?

11. I have the joy of Jesuit friendship.

One of the deepest touchstones for my vocation is my Jesuit friends. Cementing my commitment to the Order by taking final vows has for me a special emotional component that is decisively relational. Though it is an affection for God, and for the church and the Society as communal organizations, carved out from this deeply felt fondness is a piece reserved for my Jesuit brothers, especially a special group for whom I reserve the title "close friends." It is in these relationships that the ideal of community is, for me, most real. Though I live in community, it is fair to say that community will never be as open or as bonded together as I would like. From a psychological perspective, I, like others, just can't be that close with that many people. In this sense, community life is an ideal to strive for. But I can find this connection in several brothers wherein we have freely chosen to open to one another our hearts, share one another's joys, bear one another's concerns, support one another's hopes, and encourage one another's desires. To various degrees, such interpersonal occasions are found with other community members, but I know with certitude that it can be done with Jesuits I intentionally call "friends." I take very seriously the idea that we aid souls in companionship. Being a companion is something I freely chose, and every brother Jesuit has a right to make that claim on me. But as a human being it is natural that a few brothers have a special place in my heart. In a sense, this small group of friends is a touchstone for my vocation; that is, in living out my relationship with each of them, I model most fully the Society's noble ideal: our call to model a life of being friends in the Lord.

For the reader:

- How grateful am I for each of my closest friends? How do I express my gratitude to them?
- How have the friendships in my life helped to make me a healthier and holier adult?

12. Being a Jesuit helps me to grow in gratitude.

If I had to name an emotion that best captures my feelings as I finished the Long Retreat, it would have to be gratitude. As I think about it, it seems to me that as the years pass by, remaining a Jesuit means, simply, more and more becoming a "man of gratitude." In other words, I find my life increasingly defined by experiences of gratitude. As I recollect the many years of my Jesuit life, I find myself growing more sensitive to a subtle but noticeable change. Now, a grateful heart is increasingly the filtering perspective I use for understanding my personal experience. What I think, what I feel, and what I do—upon reflection, and with less and less effort on my part—flows into a growing overall sense of gratefulness. As I attend to the reasons I offer for keeping my commitment as a Jesuit, I could just as easily say I am setting forth reasons for being grateful. I now sense more clearly Ignatius's thought that, truly, all is gift.

For the reader:

- To what degree do I describe myself as a grateful person? How do I display gratitude in my everyday life?
- Do I sense myself growing in gratitude? What role do my commitments play in this growth?

Grateful Reasoning and Personal Commitment

Obviously, as a participant in the above discussion, I hope that the reader is now able to appreciate more deeply the graced conversation those few days of reflection afforded a group of Jesuit tertians. Hopefully, too, this account of what these Jesuit priests said about the Society of Jesus offers a glimpse into the Jesuit psyche and the factors that motivate men to remain faithful to Jesuit life. *Yet, the most significant advantage of reading this discussion is that this grateful reasoning is, in large measure, part and parcel of every life commitment.* When asked what it meant to live a healthy life, Sigmund Freud remarked that happiness consisted, essentially, in loving others and in having productive work. The commitments we make, both through relationships and through the activities to which we devote our lives, are the most defining features of what it means to be an authentic and alive human being. It is in the nitty-gritty of everyday life—whom we spend our time with, what we do—that we construct our identities and discover who we truly are. In a very real sense, it is only when people examine their life commitments that they are really able to define themselves and discover the meaning and purpose of their lives.

More broadly, the grateful reasons offered by these tertians as to why they remain Jesuits, though specific to their own vocations, are really reasons why any of us remain faithful to our commitments. In other words, these grateful reasons can be applied to our own lives, the people we love, and the work we do. A spouse we are vowed to, a friendship we maintain for decades, a career we take seriously, an interest we attend to faithfully—all are commitments we have made that in turn define and contribute to the core of who we are. Accordingly, it behooves us to take seriously each of these commitments and the gratitude we feel for them. To state this another way, the more we consciously probe and take seriously each of our commitments—whether expressed through relationships, ideas, or activities—the more we find not only personal contentment but also God's loving hand.

THE IMPORTANCE OF GRATEFUL REASONING FOR EVERYDAY LIFE

Let's take a few moments and examine specifically why we should practice grateful reasoning in the reality of our daily lives.

First, as the philosopher Jonathan Lear notes, human beings are "inherently makers and interpreters of meaning. It is meaning— ideas, desires, beliefs—which causes humans to do the interesting things they do."[11] When we act *meaningfully* we convey to others what we cherish and judge to be most significant. For Ignatius, who used the language of spirituality, the word *meaning* is best captured through the term *holy desires*, whereas psychologists would prefer to recast meaning most fittingly under the umbrella of *personal motivations*. Regardless of the discipline's perspective or the language we employ, gratefully reasoning about our commitments opens our souls and psyches to a more attentive awareness of who we are, what we most cherish to become, and what we most hunger to be.

Second, gratefully reasoning about our commitments most certainly reflects Ignatius's approach to discernment. Ignatius was very keen on discerning whether our major life decisions were authentic movements of God's working in our lives. For example, if we choose to end a long-standing friendship or embark upon a new career, we can find ourselves struggling. In such situations the most loving and Christ-like thing to do is often not clear. In his Rules for the Discernment of Spirits, Ignatius notes several times where it can be very helpful to examine critically the reasons for our actions. He goes on to note that when we face a major decision in our lives, personally reflecting on our reasons for the course of action we do choose can bring about significant spiritual consolation, which serves as a bulwark to the darkness and turmoil that characterize moments of desolation and confusion. Ignatius reminds us that we must actively fight the temptations that cloud and weigh down our decisions. Consciously reflecting on our grateful reasons for the commitments that we make offers one of the best possible antidotes to the stressors, insecurities, and temptations that derail our good intentions and heartfelt decision making.

Third, we often hear the phrase *head and heart* as if they are two totally separate realities. Most certainly they are distinguishable, as the head is associated with abstract thought, logical analysis, and critical thinking, while the heart is characterized by emotional intensity, intuition, and deep desire. But although it is true that the thought of the head and the emotion of the heart are distinguishable, in everyday life they exist in functionally intimate relationship. Moreover, humans fundamentally possess two distinct ways of knowing the world. The first way is more in line with the head, as viewed through daily conversation (discussing the pros and cons of a topic), the scientific method (conducting an experiment), and instructional explanations (e.g., giving directions to someone or following a recipe). The second way we come to know and relate to our world is more at home with the heart, such as telling a story, following a hunch, and finding inspiration through a favorite image. To navigate the world successfully, both ways are absolutely essential, yet we often place our trust in the second. For example, recollect a time when someone gave you an excellently thought-out and persuasive rationale for why you should choose one course of action. You listened attentively to this person's argument and admitted it seemed airtight, but you nonetheless found yourself responding, "I hear what you're saying, but I still feel...." Or consider a homily or sermon recently heard at church. Several weeks removed from the service, if someone asks what you liked about it, chances are you would remember less specific points or ideas pre-sented (the head approach) and emphasize the story you heard, the feelings you experienced, or the deeper truth or insight the sermon conveyed (the approach of the heart).

In everyday life it is typically hard to separate thought and emotion. Our thoughts are threaded with emotions; likewise, for the feelings we possess to be appropriate, we must have a thoughtful understanding of our world. Indeed, a defining feature of adult intelligence (as opposed to a child's thinking) is the capacity to fall in love with ideas. Witness an adolescent or young adult (the years when this quality first surfaces) talk excitedly for the first time about their interest in a political candidate or a cause they have embraced (such as antismoking or a green environment). They have not only embraced an idea, they have fallen in love with it!

Neuroscientists tellingly label emotionally charged ideas as "hot cognitions." Such emotionally laden thoughts are exemplified most directly through thinking about the people we most love, dwelling on ideas that excite us, and planning activities that enthu-siastically engage us. What we are really referring to, of course, are the commitments we have made, and the more we can bring to them our grateful reasoning, the more we bring together the reassuring knowledge of both head and heart. The close unity of head and heart certainly finds support in Ignatius's approach to the spiritual life. Ignatius discovered, both from events in his own life and from his own prayer, the critical importance we must give to the affective knowledge (combining head and heart) or the felt-sense we have of God's graced presence and action in our lives, which fits nicely with the grateful reasoning we are discussing in these pages.[12]

Last, we need to practice grateful reasoning simply because humans are remarkably adept at being creatures of habit. Even with our most dearly held commitments, we find ourselves succumbing to what was described in the last chapter as an autopilot consciousness. Just think of the many close relationships, whether marriage or friendship, in which the two parties begin to take each other for granted. Unless we practice grateful reasoning and consciously appreciate what we have been given through this spouse or friend, we run the risk of never truly being able to derive from the relationship all that it potentially offers. The same is true for any life commitment

we make. A Jesuit priest who doesn't periodically recollect his vocation as a gift to be treasured will suffer the same fate as a married person who fails to see the valued qualities of his or her spouse. At its
worst, failure to practice grateful reasoning leaves us stuck or with
diminished interest in our relationships. With time, two people might
simply stop communicating or the relationship might itself sour,
become brittle, or for all practical purposes evolve into a deadening
commitment in which the parties might stay married or remain
friends but the relationship itself is rendered shallow or hollow.[13]

THE PRACTICE OF GRATEFUL REASONING

How might we begin and increase grateful reasoning in our own
lives? Let's try an exercise. In the chart below are listed the reasons
the Jesuit tertians were grateful for their vocations. As we have noted
previously, these reasons are more than likely operative in most of
the significant commitments any of us make. With this in mind—

Step One. Begin by taking a commitment you have. It might be
a spouse or close friend who has meant very much to you over the
years, a career or job to which you have devoted yourself, or a hobby
or other activity that has provided you with joy and purpose. In the
line above the chart, write out a simple statement describing the
commitment. For example, "My marriage to _____," or
"Having _____ as my sister," or "My friendship with
_____," or "My work as _____." Most
people tend to think of their core commitments. Thus, spouses,
friends, and family members come readily to mind when one is doing
this exercise, as does one's state in life. Still other common choices
are one's faith tradition: "My Catholicism," or "My Lutheran faith,"
or residing in this parish or country or neighborhood. Even practicing grateful reasoning with a talent or personal interest proves beneficial: for example, "My interest in photography," or "My skills as a
coach," or "Using my organizational skills to help my neighborhood
or parish."

Step Two. After you have explicitly stated the commitment,
separately take each reason for being grateful listed in the chart, and
reflect on the degree to which the reason reflects your sense of gratitude for it, in regard to that commitment. For example, if you are
applying grateful reasoning to your marriage (commitment), consider

the link between your marriage and your health and then reflect on how much gratitude you feel for this connection. It is helpful, of course, to spend a few moments feeling the gratitude this reason evokes, thereby solidifying the head-heart dimension (affective knowledge) noted above. After experiencing the degree of gratitude generated by that reason, check the box that best expresses your gratitude intensity for how your marriage affects your health. Then proceed to the next reason for gratitude—the link between your marriage and your ability to make a difference in life—and reflect on the degree to which *this* reason has been a source of gratitude (again taking a few moments to feel your gratitude). Then check the appropriate box and so on with the remaining ten reasons.

In some cases, depending on the commitment you have chosen to consider, one or more of the reasons may not apply. If one of the reasons does not apply to the commitment you are considering or is not a source of gratitude, then simply check the N/A (not applicable) box and skip this reason. Also, since every person's life-history is unique, a specific commitment may well generate reasons beyond those listed here. If this is the case, then simply add this (these) reason(s) and proceed accordingly.

When you have reflected on each reason for gratitude, each should have a checkmark in one of the five columns (depicting accurately the degree and intensity of your gratitude) or in the N/A column.

A caution is warranted. Usually when rating something, we are evaluating it as better than something else. Please try to avoid this pitfall. Thus, when we rate one reason as providing us with more gratitude than another, we are *not* saying it is more legitimate than, superior to, or truer than another reason. We are not making a moral judgment; we are simply saying that, from our experience, this reason evokes a level of gratitude corresponding to the box checked. It is that simple! Our goal is to *practice* grateful reasoning and not to judge something as good or bad.

Step Three. After checking a column for each reason for gratitude, do the following: Take the five reasons you rated as the most significant sources of gratitude. These would be the checkmarks in column five. If there are more than five checkmarks there, choose only what you would consider the "top five." If you have fewer than five checkmarks, go to column 4 and select as many of them as nec-essary so that you have five. After having selected them, go to the darkened column on the far right and rank order your reasons for gratitude. In other words, assign a 1 to the most gratitude-evoking reason, a 2 to the second most, and so on. It might take some pon-dering but it can be done.

As before, rank ordering the five most significant reasons does not mean that the reason assigned last in significance (5) is any less true, legitimate, or valid than the reason rated as 1. It simply means that *at this point in your life* the gratitude you feel for this commitment is best expressed by these five reasons in the order you have ranked them. To be very specific: for *you*, on *this* day or week or month or year, this group of five reasons, in the order you have ranked them, speaks most to you, seems most authentic to you, and best expresses for you the gratitude you feel for this commitment in your life.[14]

Now take some time to reflect on and feel the gratitude con-tained in this set of five grateful reasons for the commitment you are considering. Just savor for however long the gratitude you feel for this commitment that these five reasons convey.

Do not lose sight of the degree to which this grateful reasoning coincides with Ignatius's perspective on human experience. In the *Spiritual Exercises* Ignatius pointedly asks the threefold question: What have I done for Christ? What am I doing for Christ? What will I do for Christ? If we examine the framework for this questioning, it becomes apparent that its linchpin resides in our *current life situation*. Implicit in this series of questions is an autobiographical scheme or what is broadly termed a life-story perspective. For anyone who "writes" his or her life story, whether it be literally with pen or more reflectively through conscious awareness, the central reality must be the *present*, which affords interpretation(s) of the past as well as expectations of the future; in essence, it configures the present with who we were and who we will become. Only a keen sense of the pres-ent-day course allows us to untangle yesteryear while we frame the future. Correspondingly, in order to envision effectively what we will do for Christ, we need to have some sense of what we have done for Christ. And both of these perspectives require grounding in the pres-ent moment in order to reconcile with our past and to dream our future. The only way fully to answer Jesus' call—"What am I doing for

RATING THE GRATITUDE FOR MY COMMITMENT

At this moment in my life, the following ratings best express
the gratitude I feel in my commitment to (as)

_____.

| | | Grateful ⇨ Most Grateful | | | | | RANK ORDER (1 to 5) |

Reasons for My Gratitude	N/A	1	2	3	4	5	
1. Enhances my health and well-being							
2. Helps me make a difference							
3. Deepens my meaning and purpose							
4. Brings joy to my life							
5. Fosters my faith and love of the church							
6. Nourishes my experiences of God							
7. Allows me to recognize God's fidelity							
8. Allows me to grow more in love and freedom							
9. Sustains my integrity							
10. Aids my spirituality							
11. Nurtures my friendships							
12. Fosters growth in gratitude							
13. Other							
14. Other							

Christ?"—requires that attention be paid to our current self-defining moments, which are always encompassed in and best reflected by the commitments we have made over our life history.

It is the felt-knowledge of head and heart best expressed through the gratitude we feel that energizes us to respond most freely and wholeheartedly to Jesus' call. Further, this gratitude-in-the-present provides the soothing balm that helps heal and brings peace to the ambivalences scattered through every life history, as we each seek to reconcile successes with failures, joys with disappointments, and hopes with fears. Likewise, it is this grateful reasoning we apply to our present commitments that allows us to dream of a future in which we can do even more for Christ as his brothers and sisters, thus forming the basis for the most authentic Christian stance to life and all the ambiguity it brings. All in all, gratefully reasoning through our commitments most ensures that we write a grateful autobiography, a most natural quality of a life striving to be Christ-like.

OTHER HELPFUL HINTS FOR GRATEFUL REASONING

Charting our grateful reasons offers a springboard for developing personal insight, thereby providing a wonderful venue for self-discovery. Try one or more of the additional exercises below.

1. Take the list of the five reasons you rated most highly. Do you detect any *pattern* to your list? How does this list of reasons help *define* you as a person? What does this list of five reasons say about you as a Christian? What does this list tell you about your needs? Your dreams? Your perspective on life?
2. Go over your chart and scan the reasons you have checked on the right of the chart (all your 4s and 5s). Ask yourself what these reasons might reveal to you about one or more of the following:
   a. Joys you have experienced
   b. Stressors you have experienced
   c. What you "need" now in your life in order to be the most loving person you can be
   d. Issues that bother you
   e. Losses you have experienced or are enduring

     f. Loves you have had or do have

     g. Struggles that weigh on you

     h. Temptations that burden you

     i. Insights you have discovered about yourself

3. Take your list of reasons and incorporate it into your DGI, which was presented at the end of chapter 1.

4. Some individuals have found great help in asking the person with whom they have a commitment (such as a close friend or a spouse) to also chart his or her own grateful reasons for the commitment. After each has completed the chart, share with one another the five top reasons you are grateful for the relationship. Few experiences in life offer more contentment than sharing with those we love our gratitude for them. Furthermore, this sharing in itself takes on a life of its own as an enduringly powerful source for ever-deepening gratitude!

5. Similar to number 4, if you are part of a Bible study or faith-sharing group, or a religious community or small Christian community, have each member chart his or her grateful reasoning in light of their commitment to the group, and have members share their responses. This exercise affords an opportunity to strengthen members' ties to the group and to discern the Holy Spirit in action through the grateful responding of each group member.

6. Take some of your grateful reasoning and incorporate it into your personal prayer. Use some of the reasons to formulate a personal prayer of thanksgiving for the commitment you have made.

7. Since some of our most valued commitments extend over many years or even decades, another helpful strategy is to develop some type of time perspective. Thus, for example, if the commitment I have gratefully reasoned about is a specific friendship or a spouse, go back to when the relationship started. Depending on the length of the relationship, develop increments of five or ten years and imagine how you would have rated the reasons during these various time spans and compare them with your most recent rating. What changes have taken place? Which reasons have diminished?

Which reasons have increased? What do these tell you about yourself and where God might be leading you?

Chapter 1 set out the "case for gratitude" and provided a daily examen we can use to become more gratitude-conscious. As we conclude this chapter, we have come to discern the importance of applying grateful reasoning to our everyday life. Both set the stage for the next two chapters, in which we explore the meaning of gratitude in greater depth. Finally, in chapter 5, we offer Jesus as the model for true gratitude and for what we are each called to become.

Chapter Three

EXPLORING GRATITUDE

It was one of those moments when you are overwhelmed with the feeling of being blessed. It was a Saturday afternoon and I was raking leaves on the front lawn. Their colors—yellow, red, and burned brown—blended together just right. I marveled at the colors, and then I looked up and saw my two-year-old daughter's face against the screen, smiling at me from inside the door. Behind her was our dog in her typical playful mood. As I peered over my daughter's shoulder, I could view from a distance my wife busy in the kitchen preparing what I knew would be a wonderful meal with friends we were having over for supper. At that instant it all came together, and I realized in a profound way how deeply grateful I was.

—Response of a middle-aged attorney to the statement:
"Describe a personal experience of gratitude."

When trying to understand gratitude, a logical starting point is to examine what we mean by it. Gratitude has a distinctive structure: it is an experience in which we feel positive about something done for us (a sense of giftedness), which usually leads us to give back. Yet, to understand fully the significance of gratitude, we need to expand well beyond its basic structure and to apply a variety of approaches.

This chapter offers four approaches for exploring gratitude. Each approach forms the basis for strategies and questions that are interspersed throughout the chapter. Let's begin with the first approach which, interestingly, stresses the opposite of gratitude.

The First Approach:
What Is Contrary to Gratitude?

Typically, most college students go through a period of uncertainty when deciding on a major. When a young adult stops by my office to chat, the conversation frequently turns to considering decisions about a suitable major or most appealing career choice. Over the course of many years, I have noticed one enduring theme that frequently shapes the initial discussion. As is so often the case, students may not know what they want to major in, but they are adamant and certain about what majors they wish to avoid! This tendency to arrive at a negative conclusion before knowing the positive occurs in many areas of life. For example, in deciding about a clothing purchase, we might consider many options while being quite clear about which styles or brands we would not find acceptable. Or we might find it difficult to decide on a gift for someone's birthday, but seldom are we at a loss on what not to buy! We seem to have a knack for ruling things out or deeming them unacceptable before shifting our focus to determine what we truly desire. Our certainty about what we don't want seems to set the boundaries of our choices, which then makes it easier to sort through the remaining options and choose one we deem acceptable.

Defining gratitude follows a similar course. In formulating a definition, knowing what to rule out offers a useful starting point. It lessens the possibilities we need to consider and helps us to focus more attentively on other distinctive qualities and attributes.

In proceeding to arrive at a definition of gratitude, I asked several groups of people to select from a list of over 250 words the ones they believed best described the *opposite* of feeling grateful. The twelve most commonly chosen words, in descending order, were:

- bitter
- resentful
- disappointed
- dissatisfied
- empty
- hatred
- hollow

- hopeless
- hurt
- sad
- vengeance
- frustrated[1]

What do these choices tell us about gratitude or, perhaps more accurately, the feeling of being ungrateful? Most of the words cluster around one of three themes. One group suggests some type of *void* (empty, hollow), another has *anger* as its theme (bitter, resentful, hatred, vengeance), and a third is best identified by its *pessimism* (disappointed, sad, hopeless). Thus, we can say that when we feel ungrateful, we sense something missing (void), we are prone to negativity (anger), and we view our future bleakly (pessimism). This word list leaves us joyless, and most likely we would avoid people who display these qualities.

In order to understand ingratitude better, I asked a group of people to describe a time when they felt ungrateful or lacked gratitude. A common theme for many was regret over missed opportunities or having taken someone or something for granted. Several people described times when their negative feelings such as anger, disappointment, sadness, or envy were so consuming, they were blinded to the blessings they possessed. Some recounted stories about attempts to cope with a devastating loss, which robbed them of grateful memories of the loved one they had lost. As one young adult noted, "I lost my love because I was ungrateful." Another person, who experienced a parent's sudden death, said that during this painful time, "I was angry, resentful, and in denial." As friends and other family members tried to be present to her and to comfort her she said, "It only caused me more anger, which I focused on them." This all-consuming loss eclipsed others' attempts to sooth her emptiness. Fortunately, with time's passing, most individuals were able to look back on their ingratitude (no doubt aided by their life experiences) and, with remorse, acknowledge their mistakes.

Ingratitude becomes a fertile breeding ground for *psychic entropy*. The term *entropy*, borrowed from physics, refers to the inevitable tendency of virtually everything to break down and disintegrate. Psychic entropy exists when consciousness is weighed down by the burdens of apathy, gloom, lack of motivation, or inner turmoil. When psychic entropy takes hold, it proves enormously difficult to maintain the positive feelings associated with gratitude.[2]

OBSTACLES TO GRATITUDE

Up to this point, we have focused on the opposite of gratitude by looking at words associated with ingratitude and then examining how people describe themselves when overcome by ungrateful feelings. The third and final method utilized to help grasp the meaning of ingratitude came from post–Long Retreat interviews with my tertian brothers. I asked each to explain what the phrase *the opposite of gratitude* meant to him.

Flushed with gratitude at the retreat's end, and having become acutely aware of God's bountiful outpouring of grace in their lives, these Jesuits were highly sensitized to what it meant to be grateful. With such gratitude, they were also likely to be highly sensitized to ingratitude. Just as knowing about goodness or witnessing a noble act sensitizes us to vice, so, too, when we are grateful we noticed the absence of gratitude all the more. To insights generated from discussions with my tertian brothers, I added the observations of others I had interviewed, as well as conclusions drawn from nearly two decades of clinical work with individuals whose lives were marked by serious personal problems, hardened emotions, and difficult life situations. The blending of these three perspectives produced ten conditions or obstacles to gratitude that are described below. As you read over these roadblocks, take the time after each to reflect on the degree to which each might hinder or threaten your own desire to live gratefully. Some ways are then offered to turn these obstacles into opportunities for gratitude.

First Obstacle: Entitlement

One person described entitled people as "self-absorbed," another as "using other people." A professional colleague told me that in her experience, entitled people were individuals best described as "myopic"—unable to see beyond themselves. Understandably, individuals who believe they are entitled ("owed something") find gratitude difficult. A sense of entitlement is frequently seen in people who exhibit narcissistic traits. Narcissists, or those individuals displaying narcissistic features, wrap themselves in their own self-importance. As a consequence of their inflated views of themselves, they find apologizing or acknowledging mistakes difficult or even inconceivable.[3] Prideful and often arrogant, they habitually exploit personal relationships to achieve self-serving goals. From the narcissist's perspective, others are objects to be used rather than individuals with whom to relate. Typically, entitled individuals convey little empathy toward others, yet indulge in distorted views of their own worthiness, thereby deserving (at least in their own eyes) nonstop admiration. Such entitlement breeds self-centeredness and a demeaning attitude that downplays or ignores the talents of others.

Genuine expressions of gratitude are rarely forthcoming from such self-absorbed individuals.[4] Needless to say, a therapy client who displays narcissistic features frequently constructs barriers in order to sabotage the building of a sound relationship with his or her therapist. In the initial stages of therapy, one clue to some form of narcissism is a client's tendency to verbalize and attach enormous significance to seemingly trivial or insignificant occurrences. At times the client carries on a monologue, leaving the therapist feeling irrelevant. One therapy client waxed eloquently on many insignificant topics and gave me the distinct message that I was there simply to listen to his endless rambling about himself and what were in his eyes significant accomplishments or crippling slights. After each session I was struck by the degree to which his world revolved around him. He was "a legend in his own mind"! After one therapy session I distinctly remember thinking he was so self-absorbed that being grateful in any meaningful way was beyond him.

Shortly thereafter, I began to reflect on the integral role gratitude played in living a happy and fulfilling life. Sadly, this sense of entitlement usually serves to mask an all-too-painful reality of an impoverished inner life, for which narcissism serves as the protective shield; indeed, narcissists, despite their outward appearances, are extraordinarily fragile. With such emotional barrenness, seeds of gratitude seldom take root.

Second Obstacle: Victimhood

"Victimhood," said one tertian, "is saying to others, 'I can't do anything alone. I will always rely on others' attention.'" Another person noted that when we define ourselves as victims we "stay in the mold of a prisoner." Today, more and more people seem to regard themselves as victims. Without dismissing the truly horrific situations of many, there is no doubt that feeling victimized by someone or something has grown socially acceptable. In such a mindset, self-understanding based on a dysfunctional home or toxic parent takes on explanatory power: "I am the way I am because of my terrible home life." Each of us in our young- and middle-adult years must construct a workable and sustainable sense of personal identity and come to a suitable answer to the question: Who am I? The response to this question is initially formed, gradually sculpted, and largely constructed by establishing relationships, achieving goals, and contributing to the wider world. One's self-identity develops within a psychological culture. One need only browse through any bookstore and notice shelf after shelf lined with books on self-help, psychological illnesses, coping strategies, and other psychological themes. Psychological perspectives, like others, have merit. The more fully we comprehend others' behaviors (for example, a child with ADD, a traumatized adult), we have deeper understanding and compassion for someone's suffering and are able to build more satisfying relationships while yet acknowledging our own or a loved one's limitations.

Nonetheless, some therapists mistakenly view all personal behaviors and attitudes as primarily the result of psychological problems. For instance, how frequently do we attribute an adolescent's problem to low self-esteem when the major issue is really the young person's failure to live up to certain standards and take responsibility for his or her behavior? Fueled by a therapeutic emphasis, some mental health professionals all too willingly cast people as victims. As a result, emotions, attitudes, and behaviors are interpreted through the narrow lens of victimhood. Within this view, traditional ideals such as character, duty, virtue, and commitment receive short shrift. As we identify ourselves more and more as a casualty of life, our capacity for gratitude withers. One person remarked that portraying oneself as a victim is like playing in a card game in which you are dealt a "bad set of cards" and refuse to do anything about your hand. One's self-identity as a victim undercuts the ability to appreciate what one is, has, or has been given and keeps one wallowing in a morass of self-pity. Unfortunately, victimhood feels good! It makes for advertising: "poor me."

More often than not, victimhood discovers a staunch ally in anger. To illustrate, a person told me about visiting an old family friend in a nursing home. Hardly in a grateful mood, the resident was fuming over an unkept promise: a month ago, a mutual friend had promised him a television that had yet to appear. His voice rose with increasing anger as he complained of his predicament and cast himself as the victim of his friend's indifference. His visitor, sensing both his anger and the satisfaction he derived from being a victim, began teasing him in hopes of squelching his irritable mood. It seemed to work! Shortly thereafter, both found themselves laughing. Then, all of a sudden, the older man ceased his merriment and said abruptly, "Stop it." My friend asked, "Why?" His elderly friend responded, "If I keep on laughing I won't be angry anymore!" Apparently, at least for this man, feeling like a victim was his best medicine, even if the side effect was misery.

Third Obstacle: Rugged Individualism

Rugged individualism encourages us to subscribe to the illusion that "we can go it alone." One of the tertians offered the image of a "closed fist or a sneer" as an apt symbol. When viewed in its extreme, an individualist's stance lacks a vocabulary for appreciating community needs and the common good.[5] On the one hand, of course, having natural talents to achieve personal success is (and should be) an ongoing source of gratitude. Hopefully, all of us are grateful for having certain abilities and for the personal accomplishments these abilities make possible. On the other hand, dwelling excessively on personal achievement creates a focus solely on personal gain that slights if not eclipses the consideration we owe others. As we reflect on our life histories, it is hard to deny that each of us to a significant degree arrives where we are in life due to the generosity of others who have loved and guided us—parents, friends, teachers, coaches, and so on. A mindset geared solely to personal achievement soon loses track of the role others have played in shaping our success. Further, unbridled self-sufficiency eclipses the fact that we exist in relationship to wider communities (neighborhoods, civic groups, and so forth). Because gratitude assumes relationship beyond one's self (acknowledging the gift-giver), a mindset excessively prone to individualism subverts human connection, thereby rendering "being grateful" a feeble if not alien experience. Individualism, though an attitude that can accomplish much, sabotages the grateful heart if taken too far.

Fourth Obstacle: Materialism

As noted in chapter 1, when life's focal point becomes dominated by acquiring material goods or accumulating money, then our capacity for gratitude erodes. If we are motivated primarily by what we can acquire or replace, then we are mentally rerouted from the gratitude of the here-and-now to the allure of future acquisitions; in effect, there always remains one more thing we must possess. This future-oriented mentality feeds on itself as we continually interpret our present situation as inadequate or feel that we have been short-changed. If we think about our gratitude moments, we discover numerous instances that are special or can be rejoiced in or cherished just for what they are, *at the moment*. Moreover, while basking in such feeling we sense in ourselves an experience of completeness. (Recall an unexpected gift or someone saying "I love you," and ask how you would describe yourself at the moment the gift was given or when those three words were shared.) When taken to heart, these basic details of the gratitude-experience contrast starkly with a mentality that ignores the moment and obsessively looks ahead to what can be gained, acquired, or possessed.

Many Americans erroneously equate greater income with greater happiness. This mistaken notion fails to consider the rapid pace at which humans become comfortable with new surroundings and events. For example, for a period of time the person might enjoy a ten percent pay raise and the salary jump from, say, fifty to fifty-five thousand dollars annually. For a period of time there will be the happiness that comes with a higher income and its increased purchasing power. As time passes, however, such satisfaction fades as our standard for evaluation adjusts. In other words, we slowly begin to forget the joy and benefits arising from the increase and slowly begin to compare ourselves to those making more than we do: "Why can't I make sixty thousand like she does?" For many, a sense of insufficiency seeps into consciousness; its lone remedy is to acquire greater pay raises that ensure more and more wealth. Thus, says author Sheila Dierks, "Americans' materialistic culture puts the emphasis on just the wrong thing—what we don't have, rather than what we do."[6] As a consequence, many loop themselves into a repeating cycle of unfailingly comparing themselves with those who have more. The only solution to these feelings of being deprived resides in devoting ourselves to acquiring even more money!

This materialistic mindset imperils the capacity for gratitude because when we preoccupy ourselves with material gain, it more often than not becomes an end in itself. Making money consumes more time and energy spent on reaping ever-greater financial reward. Such "material advantages do not readily translate into social and emotional benefits. In fact, to the extent that most of one's psychic energy becomes invested in material goals, it is typical for sensitivity to other rewards to atrophy."[7] Opportunities for gratitude shrivel when our focus and desires are based mostly on financial reward. Moreover, when money is the primary motive, the experiences that generate so much of our gratitude, such as friendship, beauty, craftsmanship, novelty, nature's wonders, discovery, and personal insight are deemed of secondary importance, not worth the time, or even irrational! Why? Because when money is *the* priority and the only "sensible" thing to acquire, the sole rational course requires that we devote our energies to attaining greater financial prosperity. When we fall into this mindset, our bank accounts might grow but the grateful life shrinks.

Fifth Obstacle: Taking It for Granted

We all know people so caught up in the moment that they miss the wider picture; a common name for this is tunnel vision. As an obstacle to gratitude, tunnel vision means we simply fail to perceive the many blessings before us. When tunnel vision takes hold, awareness of other people, situations, and the wonders of life recede. All in all, tunnel vision numbs sensitivity to the innumerable invitations to gratitude that surround us. To take just one common example, time and time again an unforeseen event occurs, or we hear or read about something that jolts or even shocks us. Reacting to such tragedy we are awakened from our slumber and begin anew to appreciate our blessings. For example, while I was researching and writing this book, several airline crashes occurred, the beloved NBC newsman Tim Russert—only in his fifties—died suddenly, and several natural disasters ravaged certain areas of the world. As a fifty-nine-year-old in good health who has flown over a half-million miles visiting over fifty American and twenty foreign cities, I was led by each of the above tragedies to stop, ponder, and appreciate my own fortunate situation. I must admit, however, that soon thereafter one or more pressures, preoccupations, deadlines, or obligations soon overtook my grateful awareness. Sadly, I soon found myself once again taking for granted my own fortunate situation.

Comparing conditions, and thus cultivating awareness of one's fortunate state, is one way to keep gratitude fresh.[8] Another is to treasure the surprise of gratitude. A middle-aged woman wrote about how the surprise of gratitude provided a new perspective when she was vacationing with a friend.

> In the late afternoon shortly after leaving the park, driving through mountains to our lodging stop, we had no idea of the surprise gift awaiting us as we turned another bend on this mountain highway. Directly in front of us, across the early evening sky, a huge, magnificent rainbow filled the expanse of sky about the mountains! I was overwhelmed with its beauty and overcome with emotion, sensing, as it were, God's love for me personally and the renewal of that divine, gratuitous covenant of love.
>
> I *knew*, in a new way, God's personal and enduring love for me, for all people, for all creation. I was filled with an awareness of all this as *free gift*—unearned, undeserved, purely free gift! There were no words adequate for a truly fitting response. But I blurted out a spontaneous "Thank-you, God. I love you, too!"

A middle-aged man shared with me his incessant preoccupation with some personal concerns. He was unsure of what the future held for him and felt paralyzed with indecision. Walking one day, he looked up and, like the woman above, he too saw a rainbow in the sky. Suddenly, he noted that welling up inside of him was the realization that his life mattered. He stated that he was struck by the immensity of his feelings and now, several decades later, he recalls this event as an example of gratitude's surprise. His new positive state motivated him to find purpose and to move forward rather than remain stuck in blinding self-absorption.

Sixth Obstacle: Manipulation

People who spend their time manipulating others are hardly likely to feel gratitude. Manipulators are rarely able to give any type of gift, whether it be a present or even a compliment, without conditions attached. Because of their power and influence, the manipulation by national leaders bears particular scrutiny. No one denies the sheer magnitude of Richard Nixon's influence on world affairs and global politics during the final four decades of the twentieth century. Notwithstanding his foreign-policy triumphs, he quickly comes to mind when one thinks about manipulative politicians. I have never come across anyone who has described the former president as a grateful person or as having the qualities associated with gratitude. Sadly, darkness clouded and suspicion poisoned his perceptions of others. Judging his enemies to be everywhere, he missed opportunities to find goodness in people. The blinding secrecy surrounding his decision making reflected an intensely introverted man with a deep distrust of others. More often than not, he either held people in disdain or viewed them as ripe for manipulation.

> And, alone, as he thought or as he watched others, he studied their words and actions and he calculated their motives. Like most of us, he could judge them only by what he knew of himself. More often than not, he thought other people were like him. But they were not. The power and opportunity of the presidency sometimes brought out the best in him, but it brought out more of the worst because he trusted almost no one. He assumed the worst in people, and he brought out the worst in them. He was too suspicious, his judgments were too harsh, too negative.[9]

When considering the effects of manipulation, most people feel its effects especially through their relationships. At one time or another we find ourselves on the receiving end of someone else's manipulative intentions. When feeling used, we grow anxious and angered, because the more we realize we are being manipulated, the more we understand how our sense of being free or in control of our actions and thoughts is compromised. Most importantly, perhaps, we come to realize that the one manipulating us had no concern for our welfare. The person's intent was solely to meet his or her own needs or to cause us harm (or both!), and we find ourselves viewing the manipulator harshly.

Each of us can identify with the above and recall some person who exploited us in one way or another. But when reflecting on the relationship between manipulation and gratitude, we should consider how we ourselves have been a force for manipulation. The temptation to manipulate is especially likely to occur when we are feeling insecure or emotionally needy, or when we find ourselves in a relationship of great emotional intensity. Recalling such instances when we have manipulated others is not pleasant, but it is vital for personal growth. Most of us, when struggling in a relationship, eventually realize what one person noted: "Sometimes one doesn't even know how to feel grateful unless one approaches another person without being possessive and demanding and allowing the other person to do the loving, and in those moments one can feel the deepest gratitude for a love that one has not controlled, a love that is freely given from the other."

Seventh Obstacle: Suffering

As we ponder the role of suffering in our lives, we are led to admit, perhaps grudgingly at times, that many of the adversities we have faced and the sufferings we have endured—whether emotional or physical—have seasoned us, provided us insight, and become integral to who we are today. Applied to gratitude, we can say the following: the soil in which gratitude is rooted always contains some barrenness. To some degree, our brokenness burdens us. When we are overwhelmed by our suffering, it can become difficult to maintain a grateful perspective. Despite such adversity, over time most of us can recollect grateful moments or even see in such sufferings opportunities for gratitude.

One middle-aged woman felt pain in the wounds she carried from a recent divorce. When asked to think of what she was grateful for, she mentioned her daughter: "I thank God numerous times for bringing this precious miracle into my life. Through all of the hard times, I still have managed to thank God every day for her." Her marriage, though the source of great pain, also led to her greatest joy.

One therapist commented she was grateful that her sessions were, in the midst of people's sufferings, a time-out period that conveys to clients that they "are not stuck." During this time-out period, gratitude serves as a catalyst that loosens the shackles of self-hatred or powerlessness that so often afflicts the traumatized and those wrestling with intense psychic pain. As self-loathing unravels, clients realize that they must put together a life that offers them a perspective on their pain. What emerges for them is a sense of hope and a growing confidence that they can go on. As this process unfolds, gratitude blooms. Unfortunately, suffering is not only a rich source of gratitude but also a poison for undermining it. Indeed, horrendous anguish stemming from imprisoning addiction, crippling physical or mental illness, or horrifying episodes of sexual, physical, or psychological abuse can so root itself in the life histories of some that their capacity for gratitude is profoundly impaired. In some cases, the staggering depths of emotional suffering can be so overwhelming that it derails almost all attempts to fashion a stable life narrative with gratitude as a significant theme.

Eighth Obstacle: Amnesia

It is said that gratitude is the heart's memory. Without gratitude, our hearts would ache. Recollecting acts of kindness from someone or instances when we were the beneficiary of another's goodwill strengthens our awareness and resolve to live gratefully. But developing a "memory of gratitude" requires significant effort. Neglecting to nurture a grateful memory breeds emotional hunger. Recall earlier that two words associated with a lack of gratitude were *empty* and *hollow*. When remembrances of gratitude fade, a feeling of deprivation surges unimpeded.

An amnesic memory around gratitude creates a breeding ground for one of life's most dreaded feelings: sadness. Among negative emotions, anger arouses us and encourages us to strike out, whereas fear makes us cautious and causes us to withdraw. Sadness—a dulling, yearning, and forlorn experience—contains an additional component. To be sure, it is an aching feeling; but it is also an emotion rooted within a unique meaning structure. Sadness at times thrusts before us the questions: "What if…?" "If only I had…." Feeling sad generates a yearning for something we wish could have been otherwise. Without this "something," we are resigned to a feeling of isolation. To demonstrate the powerful clutches of sadness, try this exercise: Simply sit quietly alone and undisturbed. Concentrate on an event, situation, or person that brings on sadness. Focus on this silent sadness. Many people can bear such introspection for a minute or two but then, suddenly weighed down by their sadness, seek relief through some kind of distraction. Given what has just been described, it is not surprising that sadness overwhelms. Gratitude, in turn, is the soothing balm for sadness. When we make the effort to recollect the past with gratitude and celebrate the goodness of our lives rather than mourn what might have been, we can more ably cope with life's challenges.

Ninth Obstacle: Lack of Reflection

As discussed in chapter 1, a growing concern in this information-driven age is exposure to a knowledge glut. Increasingly sophisticated technologies such as wireless phones, computer-generated data, and electronic mail saturate us with endless amounts of information. Yet, in the midst of the information deluge, we are expected to make wise and prudent decisions, even as the time needed to assess such choices dwindles and competing demands of various and expanding adult roles (e.g., friend, parent, spouse) require listening attentively, giving input prudently, and reacting appropriately. A friend recently described her own situation, which vividly illustrates this dilemma. She receives thirty or more e-mail messages a day, and when she travels without her laptop she frequently returns to find well over one hundred e-mails requiring her attention. At the same time, she is responsible for overseeing the decisions of her subordinates, smoothing out conflicts among them, and representing her division's interests to both upper management and other divisions within the company. On the personal level, she takes seriously her role as wife and mother, and as a caregiver to an aging parent. Like many others, she is increasingly absorbed and drained by the information she receives, the decisions she must make, and the expectations she must fulfill. Although my friend's situation may be more pressing than most, the twin realities of information overflow and juggling her numerous responsibilities all too often deplete her psychic energy and fragment her sense of control. Consequently, she experiences little opportunity for solitude and a decreased capacity for contemplation.

In such situations, finding meaningful moments to reflect upon the richness of life's blessings recedes. And yet the commitment to live gratefully requires that we set aside time for it. (All the more reason to practice the DGI described in chapter 1!) All told, humans are notorious creatures of habit, typically going about a busy day oblivious of the numerous opportunities for gratitude. In a sense, gratitude is our loyal but too-frequently neglected companion. A middle-aged man shared a story from his young adult years that demonstrated the ill-effects of ignoring the reflection borne of solitude. He described himself as having been "stuck in a rut," overcome by tiredness and malaise. Fortunately, he possessed the foresight to remove himself from the situation for a while and to spend time in a nourishing environment that afforded time for rest and reflection. "It was a time of great joy," he recalled warmly. "The essence was that I was rewarded emotionally for doing nothing. All I had to do was enjoy existence." He reaped the fruit of his decision. With renewed vigor he returned to the task before him and soon thereafter accomplished his goal. Further, what evolved from this quiet time was a perception of things and how life was now "different." This difference had both short- and long-term effects. In the short term he completed several pressing and challenging tasks awaiting him. In the long run, he remarked that the experience of gratitude had a permanent effect on him. He said, "It has opened up a space I can return to, even though I am not always in it." Though most of us do not have the luxury of carving out several weeks for reflection, all of us require a quiet place to which we can go.

Unless we set aside opportune times for playful leisure, fruitful meditation, and joyful surprise, numerous grateful moments elude us. When we make the time for reflection, we are invariably rewarded by gratitude's surprise. One man was thus surprised when attending a holiday celebration. He entered the party with a disturbing and immobilizing uncertainty about his situation. Needing time alone, he took a long walk for over an hour. During this time apart from the festivities, he thought about God and suddenly was consoled by the many possibilities before him. His gratitude to God opened up new possibilities, and he saw his situation and future in an entirely new light.

Tenth Obstacle: Negative Moods

We can see that troubling emotional states discourage gratitude. Any negative emotion impedes the grateful heart we so desire. When weighed down by sadness, preoccupied by envy, seized by anger, afflicted by guilt, or dogged by any number of other negative feelings, we shut the door to gratitude. More often than not, a negative mood distracts us from realizing the blessings before us. Recall a time when you were sad, envious, angry, or guilt-ridden. Then ask yourself: How grateful was I? Chances are, gratitude was absent and you found yourself narrowly focused on what was causing you to be sad, envious, angry, or guilty. Intensely negative moods impose blinders. We are so self-absorbed by our distress that we become stuck. Seemingly imprisoned in an emotional fog, we remain unaware of gratitude's invitation.

Having considered gratitude from the perspective of what its opposite is and what prevents it, we can conclude that to have gratitude we must make the conscious choice to cultivate it. The obstacles cited above remind us just how fragile gratitude can be, how easily it is eclipsed, and how readily it vanishes.

A FINAL COMMENT ON OBSTACLES

Although opportunities for gratitude abound, so too do the possibilities for derailment! Many of these obstacles relate in one way or another to interpersonal conflicts. For example, feeling entitled, portraying oneself as a victim, acting self-sufficient: all lead inevitably to friction in our relationships. Conflict causes a number of behaviors to surface. First, we become defensive. Second, we go into an attack mode. Third, we see the other person in totally negative terms. Fourth, we question the other person's intentions. (Just recall the last time you got in a heated argument with someone you cared about.) Though conflict is an unavoidable part of relating with others, and within limits can be a vital source for growth in, and insight into, our relationships, continual clashes and strife are a cause for concern and are toxic when our goal is to establish mutually supportive and nourishing relationships.

Gratitude serves as a helpful antidote to counteracting such discord. The Jesus we worship and seek to identify with certainly knew conflict. What is remarkable about him was his uncanny ability to absorb the painful attacks and venomous ill-will his goodness generated. While he always proclaimed the truth, his approach "took in" the loathing, envy, and insecurities that others directed at or displaced on him, and transformed such dissonance into a message of peace that was always an invitation to love. How could God-made-human respond so lovingly? As we will see in chapter 5, I believe gratitude was central to Jesus' life, and his grateful state played a significant role in allowing him to respond as he did. When grateful, we feel a sort of *surplus* in our lives that serves to absorb, and thus cushion us from, the negative events we confront daily. In a sense, gratitude creates an *immunity* that enables us to weather everyday stressors and respond with more understanding and equanimity to upsets ranging from the inconvenient to the truly hurtful. (Just recall when you were in a deeply grateful state. Didn't your gratitude lead you to be less flustered, agitated, and perturbed in both your relationships and surroundings?)

The role of gratitude in helping us negotiate successfully the ups and downs of life also points to our role in helping others in *their* life journeys. Our goal must be to invite them to gratitude by practicing the *art of gratitude*. How do we do this? We accept people where they are and we are present to them in their life journey, assuring them by word and especially deed of our steadfast respect and concern for them. And in this process of faithful journeying together, we demonstrate to them our own gratitude and, when the opportunity presents itself, invite them to gratitude by gentle comments and encouraging observations and insights.

In a similar vein, one of the primary goals of pastoral care must be to leave someone with a greater feeling of hope. Few things are more apt to do this than having a grateful heart. As such, a primary mission of pastoral care should always be gratitude-related themes as applied prudently and respectfully to a specific pastoral situation.

THE DEVELOPMENT OF GRATITUDE

Let's build on the discussion above by transforming the opposite of gratitude or the obstacles to gratitude into occasions for gratitude. Try one or more of the following exercises.

Exercise One: Transforming Obstacles into Opportunities

It has been shown that a number of negative emotions are associated with ingratitude. Let's take a number of negative emotional states common in daily life: disappointment, unhappiness, loneliness, hurt, sadness, and frustration. There are several ways to recast this negativity into positive channels for gratitude.

Scan the following list and ask yourself which of the specific negative feelings above you would associate with some troubling time or events in your life. A list of these experiences might include relating the negative feeling—

- To a past or current relationship....
- To a specific time period....
- To a place where you lived....
- To a goal you attempted and failed to accomplish....
- To a desire or dream you wished had come true....
- To someone you admired but who later disappointed you....
- To someone in authority who hurt you....

Now do the following:

- Imagine the circumstances surrounding what happened: when and where, as well as what took place.
- Spend a few moments with the negative feelings you had or even still have now. Pay specific attention to the intensity

of the feelings. Which feelings seem most prominent? Do
any cause particular upset for you even now?

- Remind yourself that you are *not* reliving the experience. It
  is in your *past* and, though it might still provoke uncom-
  fortable feelings, you nonetheless have a *perspective* from
  which you can now view your discomfort.
- Remember that we are focusing on what is contrary to gratitude. Hence, gratitude does not generally surface when
  recalling one or more of these negative experiences.
  Nonetheless, consider whether your negativity about the
  situation limited or eliminated an opportunity for gratitude.
  In other words, is it possible that refocusing on your experience now not only evokes naturally occurring feelings, such
  as sadness, disappointment, and so on, but also presents
  some opportunity for gratitude? Frequently, such gratitude
  is disguised and we must unearth it. With effort, we are
  able to discover the *surprise* of gratitude. A way to do this is
  the following. Take the example you selected above and
  the negative feelings associated with it. Now, having perspective on this situation—more life experience and the
  passage of time—ask yourself:

- What lessons has this experience taught me?
- What ability did it draw out of me that I didn't think I had
  when going through it?
- How am I more the adult I want to be because of it? Or,
  how has it helped me to become the Christian I desire
  to be?

Consider now that by answering one of these questions you
have created an opportunity for gratitude! Spend time with one or
more of your answers and just be grateful! Of course, rarely will this
gratitude-surprise eliminate the negative feelings. Your reactions to
this painful experience might have had years to fester and weigh you
down. As such, doing this exercise on gratitude will not make such
feelings vanish! However, if you can summon the gratitude that is
present in your negative feelings, then you can create a counterbal-
ance to your negativity. This "beachhead for gratitude" can go a long

way to offset or contain your negative state. As a consequence, you realize that there is more in you than just your negativity, and that in itself is a blessing to be thankful for.

In a similar vein, when we can summon the insight to discover in our negativity some gratitude moments, then the opportunity for grateful reasoning arises. Take a negative event that has been a source of hurt over the years and apply it to the chart in chapter 2. Ask yourself what grateful reasons have surfaced as a result of this pain. Respond to each of these reasons with the gratitude you feel.

Exercise Two: Recalling Significant People

Despite the cultural messages to "do it on my own," most of us find solace and comfort in recognizing our indebtedness to numerous people whose influence and kindness have helped shape who we have become. When we pause, we come to realize that the many people who have formed us reflect an immense repository of generosity. Although we might know this intellectually, we often fail to take the time to feel it or give this truth about our lives its due. Let's break the habit of taking life's blessings for granted. Rediscover the gratitude you feel toward the many people who have shaped or contributed to your life. Call to mind a specific person for each of the following, together with what this person did for you that triggers your grateful feelings.

- A parent who...
- A sister who...
- A brother who...
- A relative who...
- A friend who...
- A spouse who...
- A colleague who...
- A coach who...
- A teammate who...
- A stranger who...
- A teacher who...
- A neighbor who...
- A boss who...

Afterward, think of the person you have identified with each sentence and just feel your gratitude for him or her, one person at a time. More generally form the habit of writing down on a small sheet of paper five people you are grateful to have (or to have had) in your life and just feel your gratitude for them.[10] Do this daily. It works! As a way to counter the tendency to grow complacent with your gratitude list, reshuffle your list! Vary it by adding and subtracting several names every few days. This provides an "edge" to gratitude that keeps it both fresh and vibrant.

To ensure the benefits of gratitude, try this additional step. After recalling again one of the people you have noted above, take the time to consider: "What do I feel called to do, given what this person has done for me?" By answering this question you resolve that gratitude will not stop with you. Reroute it outwardly so that others, too, might benefit from your blessings.

Exercise Three: Relishing Roles

A third way to foster gratitude is to consider it in the context of your current life. First, ask yourself: Who am I? Spend some time simply describing to yourself the many roles in your life. As various phrases or descriptions come to mind, relish the occasions, situations, or people that have aided in bringing about these qualities that make up your self-definition. For example, as I describe myself, I come up with the following list: I am a son, a brother, a friend, an uncle, a godfather, a writer, a psychologist, a priest, a Jesuit, a professor, and a colleague. It doesn't take much encouragement to take time just to sit with one or more of these roles and feel grateful. We often take the many roles in our lives for granted; yet, each is a bountiful source of blessings we can savor if we only take the time to consider it.

Exercise Four: Creating Gratitude-Surprises

We counter tunnel vision by the surprise of gratitude. I came across this exercise in my own life and wish to share it in the hope that it might prove helpful. The university campus where I teach (Regis University) is designated an arboretum. In order to acquire this designation, the campus landscape is required to have a wide, varied assortment of trees and shrubs. Over this past year, the groundskeeping crew placed small blue-and-gold signs pointing out each tree's name (e.g., a Douglas fir or Colorado spruce). Like many people I find myself slavishly bound to a daily schedule and in so doing mindlessly (and foolishly) slight the many wonders around me. To break this habit, I have made a concerted effort to spend a minute or two each day in front of a different tree, enjoying its simple beauty. What always seems to happen is that in these brief, reflective moments I find myself surprised by gratitude—for example, by the color or intricacy of a leaf or the beauty of the tree as a whole. These simple joys are often springboards for the gratitude experience. Spend some moments refocusing your day. Find a routine that incorporates a plan allowing you to focus, if only for a few moments, on the ordinary as you discover what you previously took for granted, failed to notice, or gave insufficient attention.

Exercise Five: Recognizing Blessings

It is seductively easy to believe that the grass is always greener on the other side! As previously noted, we spend far too little time being thankful for what we have and far too much time being aware or envious of what others have. The writer Victoria Moran has developed a helpful way to counteract this.[11] First, make a list of what you have. Be honest! Include any positive features about yourself, such as health or intelligence. Then add various items—for example, such material possessions as certain clothes, paintings, car, and any financial assets. Now add to your list various relationships and the ways you enjoy leisure time, such as reading, going out to eat, or attending movies. Take the list you have made and now pretend this list belongs to someone else. More often than not, you will discover that you could easily be envious of someone who has so much! The moral of the story: be thankful for what is in your life rather than dwelling on what is missing!

Exercise Six: Attending to Surprise

We have frequently referred to the surprise of gratitude. Keeping an element of surprise helps to further gratitude's hold on us. One way to do this is to add to the DGI described at the end of chapter 1 an additional step that acknowledges various surprises. Another possibility is to create a diary in which you spend a few moments each day answering the question: How did my gratitude surprise me today? In order to further awareness as to how extensive the gratitude experience of surprise is present, it is helpful to review on a weekly basis the surprises that occurred during the previous week. This activity encourages the pleasant nature of surprise as something that we begin to seek out and, with time, to treasure.

Exercise Seven: Keeping a Gratitude Diary

Another exercise recommended by many is to create a diary in which you daily recount your blessings. Simply make the effort to record three blessings every day. After spending time savoring your day's blessings, take your list and evaluate each item by the phrase "taken for granted." A helpful way to carry out this evaluation is to rate each blessing on a scale of 1 to 10 (with ten being the extreme of taking a blessing for granted). Once a week, look over the lists and notice any patterns, that is, identify which items you are especially prone to take for granted. As the weeks go by, recounting your blessings and evaluating the degree to which you take them for granted will bear fruit. You'll find yourself more aware of your blessings and will not take them so much for granted.

Exercise Eight: Using Imagery

Still, another way to foster gratitude is an image exercise for dealing with daily stressors. All too frequently, the stress of modern life, whether at work, at home, or in a particular relationship, creates turmoil. We find ourselves stressed and distracted, and in no time the feeling of gratitude evaporates. I have recommended to clients a simple exercise to help deal with this turmoil. Sit quietly for a moment, close your eyes, and just imagine a soothing mist surrounding you. Have it cover you from head to toe and let it reach out several feet in all directions. Label this a "gratitude mist." Feel its soothing presence as it calms and refreshes you. Resolve that, when in this mist, nothing else matters—you just feel grateful. Now you have something to take with you wherever you go! Whenever you feel upset or flustered, just call upon this gratitude mist that is always with you.

No matter what is occurring around you, the mist triggers the benefits of gratitude.

Exercise Nine: Employing Technology

A final way to create a grateful state involves using the technology around us. Millions of Americans log on to the Internet and use cell phones daily. Many of us have for screen savers or as pictures on our cell phones images of family, friends, or enjoyable moments we have experienced. Develop a habit several times during any ordinary day of not only viewing these pictures but focusing on them. Spend a few moments being grateful for the person or scene depicted on the screen.

The Second Approach: Some Ideas on Gratitude

Philosophers, sociologists, theologians, and psychologists have contributed to the literature on gratitude. In the second and third approaches, we explore several ideas from this literature. Since the third approach explores gratitude as an emotion from the perspective of psychology, the second focuses on what others have contributed to understanding the nature of gratitude.

Many writers conceive of gratitude as entailing some type of duty, debt, or obligation. When we are recipients of another's generosity, cultural pressures require that we respond in an appropriate and timely fashion. Perhaps the most striking example of a duty or debt owed is our response to elderly parents (filial obligation). As it is commonly expressed, the kindness of parents toward their children requires some response of generosity. Assuming that one's parents have tried to be good parents, a natural sense of appreciation develops within the child that, with time, grows increasingly rich and complex. In essence, when focusing on a child's relationship with his or her parents, "it is nearly impossible to experience profound affirmation born of good will from another, without feeling gratitude towards them—especially when that affirmation is indispensable to one's having flourished."[12] Moreover, a child does not choose to have feelings of gratitude; rather, they occur naturally as he or she increases in awareness of what his or her parents have done.

Likewise, children can feel gratitude because they come to realize their vulnerability and the fact that their parents did not take advantage of their power over them. While there are many exceptions to this last statement, essentially a child feels a natural sense of gratitude since the parents could have acted manipulatively or harmfully toward the child.[13] One middle-aged professional spoke of the warmth that overcame him when reflecting on his parents' aging. When parents grow older, he said that you "begin to appreciate your parents more and more. See the good they leave in you. To fully appreciate my parents' goodness, I have to truly believe that there is goodness in me. In other words, I need to find my goodness within me." Perhaps this man's thought says it best. The loving care of parents plants and nourishes the goodness we come to feel. With time, as parents grow old, we generously and willingly give such goodness back.

With few exceptions, cultural expectations dictate that children show gratitude to their parents. As society increasingly ages, this attitude will most likely be tested. Documenting this development, a number of questions surface: How much gratitude should adult children show their parents? What about the cases in which extending gratitude in the form of financial assistance for home care, assisted living, and nursing-home residence places severe pressure on family budgets, thereby straining an adult child's obligation to his or her spouse or children? This is an especially pressing question in times of recession or economic downturns. In such instances we must ask the question: Does such gratitude have limits as more and more adult children wrestle with how to show gratitude to aging family members?[14] In sum, gratitude toward parents, though one of the most natural and widely experienced forms of significant gratitude, ironically may well represent for the next few decades one of the greatest challenges to showing gratitude.

In everyday life, expressions of gratitude range from the passing acknowledgment of "thank-you" for a routinely shown courtesy, such as opening a door, to the more heartfelt gratitude for a genuine kindness that someone has shown us. As already noted, associated with the feeling of gratitude is a social expectation that, minimally, the benefit received be acknowledged and, in most cases, at some point in time reciprocated. If we ignore this expectation, we run the risk of being labeled an "ingrate." Moreover, "an individual who rightly owes no one gratitude has lived a most unfortunate life; and a person who has been the object of proper good will on the part of many people but who feels no gratitude towards any of these individuals is an emotionally estranged individual."[15]

Frequently our gratitude is played out in a kindhearted deed, although not necessarily toward the person whose kindly act has helped us. For example, if a supervisor takes an interest in Rachael during her first job after graduating from college, she is most likely to remember this kindness when she, at some later point, finds herself in a supervisory capacity, so that she, in turn, behaves kindly toward those she supervises. On the other hand, if the person to whom we are grateful is in some immediate need, it is usually expected that we will respond in kind; otherwise, many would interpret our behavior as ungrateful. Obviously, "what makes a particular response 'fitting' or 'suitable' for discharging a debt of gratitude varies from context to context."[16] Moreover, a kindness shown us usually fosters respect and positive feelings toward others. More generally, "in any particular culture, many kinds of affective and attitudinal responses become appropriate in certain situations, and a well-developed moral personality is expected, as a matter of course, to display these."[17]

The philosopher Paul Camenisch expands the meaning of gratitude by linking it with the ethical life. The source for this moral stance associated with gratitude is our realization that through another's generosity we have been given a gift. For moral growth to take place, the grateful person not only has feelings of gratitude for the gift *given* but also responds to the gift *giver* in ways that signify grateful conduct. Furthermore, the grateful person exercises responsible stewardship in the use of the gift. We are required to use a gift properly, although we undoubtedly have wide discretion in how this might be done. To take an example from my own life, I recall feeling grateful to a professor who, during my graduate school years, took an interest in my work and was very supportive of my research. Upon completion of my degree, I attempted to show gratitude by taking him and his wife out to dinner at a fine restaurant. But equally important, the wisdom he shared with me and the insights I gained through my work with him have led me to show gratitude by trying

to be a "good" professor to the students I teach and to write on topics (e.g., moral development, spirituality, and empathy—and now,
gratitude) that benefit others. The grateful person, then, behaves in
a manner befitting the gift received and steers his or her life in a fashion that reflects and honors the gift given.[18]

The Third Approach:
Emotions through a Psychological Lens

When describing situations or events that lead people to be
grateful, they inevitably use such expressions as "I feel grateful to…"
or "I am blessed with…." Virtually everyone I interviewed endorsed
the position that gratitude was an emotion. To speak of gratitude as
an emotion, however, first requires some understanding of the nature
of emotion.

Part of the challenge of studying gratitude as an emotion comes
from the difficulty in defining emotion itself. As two seasoned
researchers of emotion wisely observe, "Everyone knows what an
emotion is, until asked to give a definition. Then, it seems, no one
knows."[19] The following questions support this observation. What
exactly is an emotion? Are some emotions more basic than others?
Are there "pure" types of emotions that serve as building blocks for
generating other emotions? How do we make sense of the thousands
of words in the English language that express a vast array of emotional states? Are there degrees of emotions? Do emotions blend
together to make other emotions? The list of questions could go on
and on. Though psychologists offer a variety of answers to the above
questions (and in the process disagree among themselves), no one
denies the importance of emotions. "Emotions figure so prominently
in our lives that it's hard to imagine not having them. We'd feel no
love when we saw our children; no sadness when we botched an
important job interview; no amusement when a friend regaled us
with stories of collegiate misdeeds; and no embarrassment when we
used the wrong name in addressing a colleague."[20]

Not surprisingly, although psychologists acknowledge the pivotal
role emotions play in life, there appears little consensus in responses to
the above questions. While the debates in academic psychology sur-

rounding the meaning, scope, and number of emotions need not concern us here, in order to appreciate more the emotion of gratitude we need to highlight the fundamental characteristics of emotion.

Typically, emotions involve brain reactions as well as bodily sensations. For example, when fearful, we are aware of our heart pounding and our rate of breathing increasing. When joyful, we sense a lightness to our bodies and a deep sense of relaxation. When surprised, we might describe ourselves as being jolted. In addition to such physical sensations, emotions involve a variety of thought processes. When we evaluate a situation as dangerous, for example, we feel fear, whereas in the presence of a close friend we assess our condition as secure, and we settle comfortably into a relaxed state.

Because emotions dispose us to action, we associate specific behaviors with certain emotions. This appears true especially for negative emotions. Fear, for example, leads us to be vigilant, to flee, or, when trapped, to defend ourselves. Anger signals us to take the offensive; it arouses us to respond intensely with reactions ranging from irritation to rage. We ordinarily so associate specific behaviors with particular emotions that we are expected to give an unambiguous response. Thus, we naturally expect someone who is frightened to proceed cautiously or to flee, or a sad person to shed tears or to withdraw from day-to-day events. The association of certain emotions with particular behaviors is best proven by the exception. For example, we register surprise or even shock when someone acts contrary to established norms and customs,[21] and thus would be dismayed if someone were to act carefree and laugh aloud in the middle of the funeral service for his or her best friend!

Emotions include other features as well. We interpret them positively (as pleasant) or negatively (as unpleasant). Further, an emotional state can be fleeting or prolonged and can be experienced within a wide range of intensity. We can be mildly amused, happy, or ecstatic, or can fall into a nearly uncontrollable state of giddiness and frenzy in which we lose all sense of composure. Anger, likewise, can show itself in avoidance, irritation, a mild agitation, pronounced upset, verbal abuse, rage, or physical assault. Furthermore, many psychologists associate particular facial expressions with specific emotions.[22]

More broadly, emotional expressions not only convey information about an individual, but also reveal the customs of one's culture.

Generally speaking, Western societies highly value individuality and self-expression. Most Americans, for example, would think nothing of expressing anger or upset. Some Asian cultures, on the other hand, discourage such public display of negativity, prizing instead harmony and consensus building. In addition, some traditions more than others encourage expressions of gratitude.[23] From a historical perspective we could even speculate as to the relevance of gratitude as a cherished cultural value. For example, would a Greek in the age of Homer or a Samurai in sixteenth-century Japan cultivate or even acknowledge gratitude as we understand it today? The loyalty of the Samurai is legendary, but was that loyalty also an expression of gratitude? And what of the ancient Greek soldier?

Emotions, of course, serve many functions. For one, they forge our individuality. An emotional experience informs us of our uniqueness ("No one could love you the way I do"). More starkly, consider life without them! Devoid of emotion, life would be sterile and daily experience dulling. Emotions, too, enhance through the way they add complexity to our lives. We sense ourselves richer, more complete, and more aware because of the special nature we affix to some emotional experiences. Technically, one might argue that the phrase *emotional experience* is redundant because every experience of which we are aware more than likely contains some feature of emotion. Further, emotions help us adapt to all kinds of unforeseen events. Thus, whether it is the wonder of novelty, the grief at loss, the joy of success, or the fear from a perceived threat, we are able to cope better with our situation because of our emotional reaction. Furthermore, emotions communicate to others our interests and concerns. A store clerk's slight, for example, might prove a mild irritant, but being ignored by a close friend arouses our anger. In this instance, the friendship evokes a stronger negative reaction precisely because of the significance we place on our friendship. To elaborate, this anger unambiguously clarifies that the relationship with our friend is vital for our well-being. Hence, we feel anger at the slight.

Emotions communicate enormous information about who we are. The people, actions, or situations that evoke emotions such as love, anger, guilt, sadness, or joy disclose our intentions and whatever we prize most significant for our lives. "Emotions accompany and enrich understandings, and they convey far more authentic information about a person's position in a dispute than any well-articulated thoughts. In ordinary circumstances, emotions instruct and energize action."[24] At the same time, it remains imperative that we handle emotions as if they were double-edged swords. When felt too intensely or expressed inappropriately, they frequently derail us from achieving our goals, disrupt our reasoning, and undermine common sense. These are just some of the reasons why the study of emotion is fascinating.

In the specific case of gratitude, as with emotions in general, the rules and customs of any culture guide the displays of emotion. In Japan, the commonly used expression *sumimasen* conveys both apology and the feeling of thanks, a concept that baffles Americans.[25] In a similar vein, in the Tamil culture of southern India, verbal expressions of thank-you are uncommon and emphasis is placed not on an interior feeling of gratitude but on the very act of gift-giving itself. "The major form in which Tamils show their gratitude for something given them is by giving the appropriate return gift, at the appropriate time and in the appropriate form."[26] In the United States, among some Native Americans, ordinary expressions of gratitude are rarely shown simply because one is expected to fulfill one's duty and honorably discharge one's obligations.[27]

As pointed out at the beginning of chapter 2, the word *gratitude* originates from the Latin *gratia*, meaning "grace," "graciousness," or "gratefulness." "As a psychological state, gratitude is a felt sense of wonder, thankfulness, and appreciation for life."[28] Gratitude can be viewed as an interpersonal emotion because its focus is directed toward someone else. In addition, we assume that the person toward whom we feel grateful acted well-meaningly and for our benefit. Such a positive feeling is apt to lead us to feel esteemed and loved.[29] Thus, a person who feels grateful is likely to feel loved and cared for by others. From this wider perspective, we see the critical role that empathy plays in the gratitude experience and the subsequent feelings of contentment and love.[30]

In one of the more extensive treatments of gratitude, Richard and Bernice Lazarus characterize gratitude as belonging to what they term the "empathic emotions"—emotions that in one way or another trigger empathy. According to these authors, emotions arise because of two processes. First, they stem from our personal meanings, which include our beliefs about ourselves, our situation, other people, and the world that surrounds us. Second, each emotion has its own dramatic plot. The personal meaning we apply when we feel grateful is that of a gift generously given to us with no strings attached. Our benefactor is someone who has our best interests in mind and has provided us with the gift solely for our benefit. The gift can be any number of things, such as emotional or financial support, time, advice, or some type of personal sacrifice made on our behalf. Gratitude's dramatic plot comes into play when we actually take the time to appreciate an unselfish gift.[31]

In order to focus on the positive features of gratitude, I asked the same people who had previously identified words they had associated with gratitude's opposite (mentioned at the beginning of this chapter) to use the same word list and choose the ones "that best describe you when you feel grateful." In descending order the words most chosen were:

- appreciating
- peaceful
- love
- warm
- inspired
- reassured
- respect
- satisfied
- joyful
- giving
- friendly[32]

How might we describe someone who possesses most or all of the above attributes? An immediate word that comes to mind is *content*. Certainly anyone we know who possesses several of the above features is most likely a contented human being. At the same time, it must be pointed out that gratitude can occur along with other emotions, even negative ones. For example, I can be grateful for the life of my deceased father while feeling sadness over his passing.[33] Mixed emotions are easily seen in moments of nostalgia. We recall with gratitude a period from our past but simultaneously are well aware of the angers, fears, or insecurities evoked by such recollected moments.[34]

All in all, gratitude is viewed overwhelmingly as a highly desired state. Further, it usually involves some type of relationship in which we recognize that we have been the recipient of someone else's gracious generosity. Usually gratitude has a positive effect. We find ourselves more open to the world around us and are frequently inclined to give back in some way to someone. When grateful, we feel gifted, and we experience an inner esteem and serenity because of the benefit that has come our way.

The Fourth Approach: The Occasions and Effects of Gratitude

In the fourth approach for understanding gratitude, we examine its occasions and effects. Although even small gestures of human thanks, such as writing a letter, offer the possibility for deriving positive benefits,[35] it is the more enduring blessings of gratitude that demonstrate its powerful appeal and lead us to prize it so highly. The following story shared with me by a man now in his twilight years is a fitting testament to the lasting influence of gratitude.

> About twenty-five years ago I fell asleep while driving in the middle of the night on a winding road through the mountains. When I hit the guard rail and was rudely awakened, I knew it was not a blowout for I had brand new tires on the car. I knew I had fallen asleep; I knew I had hit the guardrail and that I was going to be cut in two, that it would hurt an awful lot but would not take long; and I knew I was going to die and thought that was too bad because I was not all that old. When I managed to get the car under control and brought it to a stop on the right side of the road, I felt as though I had died, and that was too bad, but I was still here somehow and so I was an "extra hand" and was free to do anything, anything at all. The sense of freedom was exhilarating, for before the crash I had not been "free to do anything, anything at all."

Accompanying it, as far as I recall, was a sense of gratitude, gratitude that I was alive but most of all gratitude that I was free. That feeling was quieter than the sense of freedom, gentler, less obvious, yet real. If it glowed, it was a quiet glow, yet intense in some sense, a quiet response to receiving something I did not deserve, perhaps accompanied by a little shame at my undeservingness, a quiet response to God's fidelity in spite of my own infidelity. The sense of freedom, of being extra and so now available for anything, was the main experience; it was strong, profoundly *felt*, and lasted for a long time. As the years passed, the *feeling* has disappeared, but I think the freedom is still there. The gratitude, of course, has long been quiet, but I think it is still there, too. When I told people about the accident, they often replied, "God must have something in mind for you to do," and I would reply that I had no sense of that, but only of being free, available for anything. I do not know whether what I am doing is what "God had in mind," only that I enjoy it and am grateful to be doing it.

The gift of freedom described above is one of the many positive consequences that gratitude offers. In exploring the responses from numerous individuals, I was struck by the sustaining force for good created by the gratitude experience. As I read the many replies describing the influence of gratitude, I was reminded of psychologist Dan McAdams' description of the "nuclear episodes" interwoven within the human life story. According to McAdams, as a person increasingly understands his or her evolving life story, that person quite frequently remembers specific moments that were life's high, low, or turning points. The value of nuclear episodes rests not so much in what actually took place but in what the recalled memory symbolizes.[36] Memories of events or situations that elicited a clear sense of gratitude qualify as nuclear episodes because they described either high or turning points in life. Furthermore, the themes consistently associated with these episodes were positive ones, often centering on *goodness*. In the above example, a near-fatal accident became a liberating experience that allowed for a newly discovered freedom to do God's work. The threading of gratitude through this near-death experience (nuclear episode) prioritizes it as a pivotal event, but equally important, it has nurtured and sustained an outpouring of goodness for more than a quarter-century.

OCCASIONS FOR GRATITUDE

One way to explore gratitude is simply to ask people about their gratitude experiences—the occasions when they felt grateful. I instructed several groups of people to close their eyes and use a breathing exercise to induce relaxation. They were then asked to recall an experience of gratitude and just be with the experience as they pictured it in their mind. For the two minutes that they imagined their experience of gratitude, phrases such as "feel your gratitude" or "just be with the gratitude" were repeated slowly. After two minutes, participants were asked to open their eyes and write about the source for their gratitude. They then examined their responses to pinpoint what occasions or experiences caused their gratitude.

As you read each of the following occasions for gratitude, you are invited to write down one of your own. Spend a few moments being grateful for what you read, recall, and write about.

Gratitude's First Occasion: Family Interaction

Not surprisingly, many participants discovered gratitude through family encounters. One woman in her midtwenties said that her "experience was a deep, heartfelt gratitude for a warm, loving family, from the eldest grandparent (or great-grandparent) to the youngest grandchild (or great-grandchild)." One mother spoke affectionately about the gratitude she felt for her daughter. "We were sitting in the car going for a drive, listening to music. Every song is 'her' song. This is something we do twice a day, and this is time that we are together by ourselves. She likes to kneel and sing into the side rear mirror." Another individual retold his experience of celebrating Father's Day with his father and the rest of the family. That evening, when alone, he sat down and became flooded with thoughts that reflected his appreciation for his father. The man went on to note that these thoughts flowed into many warm memories of his deceased mother as well. In a similar vein, a nurse-practitioner shared the fondness she had toward her mother. "In all, I am grateful that my mom is the person she is and that she raised me the way that she did because that is why I am the person I am today, and how can I be anything but deeply grateful for those gifts?"

ॐ The following is a particular instance of gratitude experienced in my family that to this day makes me grateful:

_____

_____

_____

_____

Gratitude's Second Occasion: Friendship

Another major source for gratitude was friendship. One business executive recounted the support he received from friends after being falsely accused of a crime. "I felt deeply grateful that I was blessed with a close circle of friends that I was able to confide in." He went on to say, "I weathered this storm not by telling the world that I had been wronged, but rather by looking for help and guidance within a select group of key people. My overall gratitude and thankfulness to those people is so vast, I can never see myself being able to repay the favor." Another person spoke about his mother's friends. His father had recently died of cancer. He remarked how his mother's many friends rallied around her to help her bear her loss. "Even in the midst of my own mourning," he stated, "I felt that I had to make a special point of thanking those who especially helped my mother. I bought some thank-you cards and wrote individuals who had been so special to my mom. I felt that I was just giving a little bit back to them for all that they had given me."

ॐ Below is the list of friends in my life for whom I am most grateful:

_____

_____

_____

Gratitude's Third Occasion: A Stranger's Kindness

One individual told the story of a trip taken with a friend to Oregon. The friend lost control of the car and it "careened over an embankment into a ditch. Blood was gushing down my face and my friend suffered a pelvic injury." The car landed in a three-foot stream. Several minutes later a stranger appeared to offer help. He called the police and an ambulance. After they had received medical attention at the hospital, the policeman told them that the stranger and his wife had offered their home for the night. The policeman drove them to the house. Although it was around midnight, there was food waiting for them. The strangers said they could stay as long as they wished. And through bloodied sheets caused by cuts and many home-cooked meals, they remained several days. Recalling these events, the person said, "Both of us felt a deep sense of gratitude for this couple. We felt some disbelief. How could they be so kind to strangers?" The kindness offered by their hosts "shaped the way I gave to people in times of need. I felt that the only way that I could repay them was to offer my assistance to other people."

Similarly, a lawyer in his later years shared the story of a stranger offering him and his wife help when their daughter was diagnosed with Hodgkin's disease. A young couple at the time, and filled with fear for their ill daughter, they discovered through a friend a medical center that specialized in treating the cancer threatening their daughter's life. While they were standing in line at the airport for their tickets, a total stranger came up to them and stated that he was a Hodgkin's survivor. He walked them to the gate, gave them a book about wellness, and talked reassuringly to their daughter. "To imagine that someone whom we did not know would be so empathetic, so thoughtful, so kind…to greet three people he had never seen before, simply overtook us all with emotions difficult to describe. But one emotion that was crystal clear was the gratitude that we felt that evening and began to appreciate even more as we began to experience the pain of our daughter's illness and treatment, which he knew only too well." Speaking of the impact this experience had on him, this father volunteered the following: "This experience has caused me to develop a heightened sense of empathy for those who have not been blessed with good health, or who encounter some other type of misfortune in their lives. We have tried to emulate the extraordinarily thoughtful act of kindness displayed."

  Below is an instance in which I was grateful because of a stranger's kindness:

_____

_____

_____

_____

Gratitude's Fourth Occasion: Escape from Physical Harm[37]

One person described hiking toward a gorge, and on the way down from the hike she "slipped and started sliding toward the bottom." Only a large tree root shielded her from a dangerous fall. She still has a scar that reminds her of that day and of the gratitude she continues to feel for escaping the situation unharmed. Another person recounted a day when she was in a hurry. Having not scraped her windshield well, she encountered the double disadvantage of dirty car windows and the glaring sun. Late for her appointment, she continued driving but felt increasingly "helpless and out of control." Finally, when visibility became nil, she abruptly pulled over and to her surprise found her car by a sidewalk as small children were walking past on their way to a local elementary school. To this day she recalls her gratitude in not having an accident or hitting any of the children. Finally, a sales rep recounted his own harrowing experience of veering into a truck but escaping without injury. "Nobody knows why bad things happen to good people," he remarked. "It is just a part of life. I am grateful because I know how special life is."

  Below is an instance in which I am grateful because I escaped a situation that could have caused harm to me or another person.

_____

_____

_____

_____

Gratitude's Fifth Occasion: Success

Examples from individuals who found gratitude in some type of achievement included reaching a goal, winning an award, achieving an athletic victory, being accepted into a program, and getting a specific job. A man in his thirties recalled his down-and-out state while working for minimum wage. He "kept the faith," he said, and "through my hard work and perseverance I slowly moved up the ladder into middle management where I am now." His determination and perseverance was a source for his inner pride.

&? The personal success described below is something I am grateful for:

_____

_____

_____

_____

Gratitude's Sixth Occasion: Comparison

This might include exposure to another's deprived situation— for example, encountering misfortune such as poverty or illness and comparing it with one's own good fortune.[38] A student spoke about an elderly woman whose meager income left her near poverty. This student had recently moved into a simple, bare apartment and spoke gratefully about her new living space. As a member of her faith community, she had volunteered to visit the older woman. She was surprised by the impoverished living conditions but was even more struck by how grateful the woman was even for what little she had. The student left with the thought of how blessed she was for the many advantages she had in life. She noted, "I felt so grateful that I almost had to cry. I asked myself why I was so blessed while others were happy with so little. I felt bad about ever complaining." She went on to say that, as a result of this experience, she recommitted herself to spending time helping the elderly.

In another example, a physician's assistant shared an experience she had on a medical emergency rotation. She walked into a room to suture a man's face, only to discover "that he didn't have a face." Apparently, the man had tried to commit suicide. She smiled and attempted to act nonchalantly. Ill at ease, she excused herself from the examining room to speak with her supervisor and shortly thereafter returned. She and the man struck up a conversation that had a deep impact on her. After retelling the experience she concluded, "I was very overcome by it all and by how he started to open up to me. I think about him a lot and the obstacles that he faces, both mentally and physically. I am incredibly thankful that he put a lot of things in perspective for me and has helped me appreciate what I have been blessed with."

🐟 The following is a situation in which I encountered misfortune that, in turn, led me to be more aware of my blessings:

_____

_____

_____

_____

Gratitude's Seventh Occasion: Finding Good in Misfortune

Another source of gratitude can be the ability to find some benefit in a personal setback, such as growth or insight, a new way of viewing the world, or an inner strength whose realization came only after the incident. In other words, some persons found a "benefit" in what was originally viewed as a highly negative event.[39] Several individuals spoke, for example, about their addiction to drugs or alcohol. One college professor related that "somehow one's actions and conduct are related to a sense of gratitude—perhaps they flow out of a deep-seated awareness of the giftedness of being human and being alive. I have felt much gratitude lately, having surpassed six years of sobriety, and I also have considered what I meant about my sponsor's beaming face that exuded gratitude." Building on this comment, it is interesting to note that some individuals who acknowledge an addiction express gratitude for it. With passing years they view it as being a gateway for personal insight flowing from their recovery, which involved sponsors, group support (e.g., AA), personal prayer, and inspirational reading.

⁂ As I look back on my life history, I recall the following painful event or hurt that, with time, allowed me an opportunity for gratitude:

_____

_____

_____

_____

Gratitude's Eighth Occasion: Surprise

Gratitude may arise from an unanticipated development that proves beneficial. A computer programmer, for example, spoke of the difficult relationship he had with a coworker. He described their relationship as "acrimonious and bitter at times." One day, the unexpected experience of healing occurred as a result of a conversation they had in the hall. Over time, he became the recipient of kindness from his colleague. Their once-difficult relationship grew into a deep friendship. Reflecting on this conversation years later, he said, "Over time this feeling did grow into gratitude, heartfelt and lasting." The gratitude grew into friendship and friendship grew into even greater mutual respect and understanding. Another common theme of surprise was meeting someone who became a deep love or having a loved one help or do something that was not expected. In both types of instances there was a sense of gratitude.

⁂ Below is an event from my life that has shown me gratitude's surprise:

_____

_____

_____

_____

Gratitude's Ninth Occasion: Spiritual Experience

In one particularly moving story, a man recounted how God's love had been a steadfast support in a time of emotional upheaval.

Several months ago I was going through a personal crisis, during which I kept in contact with several friends. At the end of one conversation, one friend said to me, "Remember, no matter what happens, God loves you." I thanked him for this comment, though at the moment I did not consider his words further. Later that evening, however, those three words, "God loves you," became for me a pivotal prayer. Repeating those words several times, I experienced an overwhelming sense of God's love. For a brief period the anger and hurt I felt began to recede. I experienced a new way of seeing. A stream of feelings and memories soon poured into my mind. I felt a great sense of consolation as I reflected on and felt again the numerous times God has cared for me and shown me his love.

What transpired over many subsequent months was an intense struggle. My own darkness, manifested through wounded self-esteem and self-pity, led me to interpret my life history and my immediate situation in a self-serving way, which led further to a narrowing attitude, hardened feelings, and emotional upset. Fortunately, after months of intense struggle, gratitude slowly prevailed. Though still able to recognize my legitimate hurt and anger, I found that with time my "eyes were opened"; the darkness that for months had clouded my life gradually gave way. I felt truly loved—indeed, I felt I was someone special in God's eyes. God had radically touched my life.

❧ The following spiritual experience from my life moves me to gratitude:

_____

_____

_____

_____

Gratitude's Tenth Occasion: A Personal Quality

One person noted, "The thing I am most grateful for in my life is the fact that so far I have enjoyed good health." In another example, an athlete stated that his gratitude seemed "egocentric" since he referred only to his physical talents. Yet, he was clearly proud of his gifts and said that he was "grateful to be given the abilities to play and be the best I can be."

& The following personal qualities are the ones for which I am most grateful:

_____

_____

_____

_____

EFFECTS OF GRATITUDE

Having shared occasions that triggered their gratitude, these individuals were then asked to write about how they were "different" because of their gratitude—what were the effects of being grateful. Five effects were identified. For most people, gratitude frequently was connected to more than one positive outcome. After reading about each benefit, spend some moments recalling how your own life has profited from the gratitude you have felt.

Gratitude's First Effect: Maturity

Gratitude leads to increased maturity. As one student remarked: "I felt more like an adult." Or a person acted more responsibly, as evidenced by one respondent who altered his lifestyle in a way that reflected taking greater responsibility for his actions.

& When I feel gratitude, how am I more like the adult I wish to be?

_____

_____

_____

_____

Gratitude's Second Effect: Inspiration

Gratitude frequently leaves people inspired. One person remarked how his gratitude made him strive to become a better person. Speaking about his gratitude for a memorable conversation with a family member, he disclosed: "It has made me try to become a better person in school, work, and in life in general."

& How has my gratitude inspired me?

_____

_____

_____

_____

Gratitude's Third Effect: Insight

Another positive consequence of gratitude is the recognition that one has gained insight. A common word used by many was *realized*, or a phrase such as "not taking something for granted anymore." Other examples included themes of knowing oneself better or discovering the "blessings in what I have."

& What personal insights has my gratitude led me to?

_____

_____

_____

_____

Gratitude's Fourth Effect: Positive Behaviors

In many instances individuals reported that their gratitude increased their generosity and sensitivity toward others. Many people reported altering their behaviors in order to respond more lovingly or to have greater understanding.

  In what ways has gratitude increased my understanding of, and sensitivity to, others?

_____

_____

_____

_____

Gratitude's Fifth Effect: Positive Emotions

Gratitude is not only a positive emotion, but it also helps increase other positive emotions. For some, a consequence of gratitude was an overall increase in positive emotions; for example, gratitude encouraged more hopefulness or a greater sense of happiness. Still others reported a diminishing of negative emotional states, such as less worry or anger.

  What emotions do I feel when I think of my most grateful moments?

_____

_____

_____

_____

Adding to the above results, I engaged in a series of wide-ranging discussions with colleagues and friends (individuals in their midthirties and above) regarding how gratitude had affected their lives. As a result of these conversations, four additional effects surfaced.

Gratitude's Sixth Effect: Dependency

The word *dependency* receives a bad rap. In part, this negative view comes about because of the self-help movement's reliance on the term *codependency*.[40] In addition, in a society where "dream your own dreams" and "do your own thing" are given priority, being dependent is judged unfavorably. Yet, healthy dependency is vital for sound functioning. When viewed in its proper context, being dependent reflects a naturally occurring reliance we must have. An individual who occupied a position of authority described a situation he had encountered in a business setting. Needing to divert his attention to another matter, he asked his assistant to take over a specific task that normally fell under his own domain. Seeing the results of his assistant's successful handling of this additional duty, the supervisor said that his assistant's competence had put him at ease. He felt "...great appreciation for him afterward. He has truly been a 'Godsend' for me" and for this, "I am grateful."

Healthy dependency leads to interdependence. A colleague reported that his position led others to depend on him, yet their dependency in turn led him to show "less of my ego and the need to depend on others." A moving example of this interdependence was the comments of a father recounting his care for his son. This parent described how several years earlier in the middle of the night he was awakened by his son, who with urgency told him, "I'm gonna throw up." Before reaching the bathroom the child, true to his word, did just that. After cleaning up both his son and the mess, the father recalled that "oddly enough" as he went back to bed he felt grateful. Reflecting on this experience, later the father realized that his gratitude led him to the insight that there was "a reason for me." Similarly, another person, unmarried, spoke about the messy but fond memory of changing the diaper of his niece whom he was babysitting. He told how "in some way" it made him feel grateful. This "way" came about as he realized how the responsibility of caring for his niece brought out his "love for her." In both instances, ironically, a warm sense of interdependence emerges. Vulnerability (the child's dependence) meets a source of strength (a care giver) and interdependence is born.

A touching example of this interdependence was offered by a middle-aged woman who had moved into a new apartment:

> As I stood there looking around, I realized that almost everything in that apartment had been given to me by others. Much of it was from my family but some things were from friends, coworkers, and the families of students I had taught. What I saw (looking around my apartment)

were material things like furniture, books, pictures, and so on, but those material things got me to remember all the nonmaterial gifts I had also been given by these same wonderful people. I thought back on my childhood and how the only way I could have grown was if others had helped me and provided for me along the way. I was truly grateful to God and all those people for everything they had given to me and done for me.

When asked to describe the effects of her gratitude she said:

I looked at myself in a new way also. I realized my inter-dependence with others and that I couldn't and hadn't lived life on my own. Many have needed me through the years, but I have needed them, too. I think it made me less egocentric. It was easier to say to myself that I didn't need to do everything for myself.

Pause from your reading and reflect on your own reaction to the word *dependency*. American culture is more apt to champion indi-vidualism and self-sufficiency. Yet, when dependency was discussed within the context of gratitude, many people insisted that it was not something to shirk or deny but a reality eagerly embraced.

❦ Whom, in my life, am I dependent on, and how grateful am I for having this dependence in my life?

_____

_____

_____

_____

Gratitude's Seventh Effect: Greater Awareness

Closely related to the dependency people reported is recogniz-ing and being sensitive to what one person stated as "things out there." When feeling grateful, "I treasure things more," reported one person. Another spoke about the sense of "awe and wonder" that goes with feeling grateful. Still another said that her gratitude led her to "the good out there," wherever and whatever it might be. Gratitude encourages all of us to acknowledge goodness wherever and whenever we might find it. Melanie Klein, a famous psychoanalyst of the mid twentieth century, once remarked that "gratitude is closely bound up with generosity."[41] Individuals who feel interiorly a sense of their own goodness appear to possess an integrity that flows outwardly; they claim that a fundamental stance of goodness exists in the world. For them, the world is an inviting place that encourages them to spread and give away their own goodness.

&? When I feel grateful, how would I describe my view of life, other people, and the world?

_____

_____

_____

_____

Gratitude's Eighth Effect: More Than Enough

For some, feeling grateful led to inner fulfillment and interior peace. The fruit of this internal state was aptly described by one person in this way: "The more you realize how grateful you are, the less you need." As the reader might recall, two words used to describe the ungrateful state were *empty* and *hollow*. From a clinical perspective, I suspect there is truth to the belief that when lacking sufficient gratitude, some people "fill up" (or distract themselves) with possessions or act out certain behaviors (e.g., addictions) to fill the inner void. Another aspect of this fullness is its enduring quality. Gratitude's fullness, like a good friend we've grown comfortable with, gets better with age, offering an increasing amount of security and contentment. Its sustaining power allows us to acknowledge and respond more freely to our interior desires, while strengthening us to resist external pressures. Gratitude, when deeply felt, burrows within us, becoming in the process an ever-reliable wellspring from which we draw and find contentment. It seems there is always "plenty of it." One middle-aged man described a situation several years past in which he was unexpectedly asked to give an important speech. The speech was received quite positively, and afterward he received numerous congratulatory cards and comments. What was most interesting, he remarked, was the enduring power of his gratitude.

> The experience of gratitude was not a one-time transient experience. I felt it deeply when I read some of the cards and letters I received and as I reflected on my experience. There were times during the weeks after the talk when I felt it most deeply. I can think of one day while I was jogging and thinking about the response to my talk. But for the most part, the experience was a deepening and ongoing experience of gratitude.
>
> The feeling of gratitude has not left me. It has been a couple of years since the speech, so obviously I do not think about it much anymore. But the sense of gratitude I felt so deeply has been incorporated into my identity. It is now part of me rather than something I feel or think about on a day-to-day basis. I still feel the sense of responsibility and commitment that was a natural outgrowth of the gratitude experience.

Another person spoke of his thoughts after a near-fatal accident. Years later, after retelling the story of the accident, he alluded to a life incomplete. "As I look back over my life—like most lives, very incomplete—sudden death on the highway would have made sense, with unfinished business everywhere, especially within me." Now, soon to enter a nursing home, he said that to go there is simply an "added attraction." Even though his life remains unfinished, the gratitude he has felt over these many years, beginning with the accident, makes his entire life feel like it is filled up with "gift."

  In what ways has my gratitude provided me with a sense of fulfillment?

_____

_____

_____

_____

Gratitude's Ninth Effect: An Open Mind

Being grateful enabled some to venture beyond personal biases and preconceived notions. One woman expressed her gratitude for someone she knew who had crippling arthritis. Prior to her speaking with him, she had a sense of him as an invalid, trapped by his disease. She was pleasantly surprised, however, to discover that instead of wallowing in self-pity and constantly complaining, this man displayed a joyful spirit and humility. She stated that his display of nobility in the face of adversity had what she described as a "spillover effect" on her. His response to his infirmity had offered her a "stepping stone," enabling her to open her eyes and see what she referred to as the "unbounded generosity" of others.

Another person told the touching story of the marriage difficulties he was having. He had the preconceived notion that none of his friends would listen. As it turned out, he had simply misjudged at least one friend. This friend "seemed to have noticed" that something was bothering him and invited him on a hike. This friend shared the pain he had gone through in his own marriage. Caught by surprise by this revelation, the man stated: "His revealing his trouble to me helped me to open up to him. It was good to be trusted with his secret and I felt, and still feel, grateful." When grateful we can be more attentive to others' perspectives. We are not as threatened by the unknown and can more freely risk ourselves in ventures and projects that provide and create meaning both for ourselves and others.

A movement gaining ground in higher education is "service learning." Its effects offer a prime example of how gratitude can pry open our preconceived notions of life. I have witnessed several instances of this phenomenon that go more or less like this: A student volunteers at an inner city school or a home for the underprivileged. Prior to volunteering, the student sees his task as sharing his talents and knowledge with those in need. Gradually, however, as he spends more and more time in his placement, the student's eyes are opened as he becomes more familiar with the life situations of those less fortunate. Originally this student volunteer approached his work with the attitude that "I am going to help them." The more he volunteers, however, the more he begins to admire others for the struggles they endure, and he marvels at their strength and courage as they withstand heartache and tragedy. Gaining insight, he begins to consider views and perspectives beyond his own. When I interview these students as their volunteer service comes to a close, the attitude shift is remarkable. What is at first thought of as a duty is now viewed as a privilege, for the student recounts how grateful he now is for having had the experience that has taught him new ways of viewing his world. This student-teacher has become the *teachable* student.

🦋 What are the ways in which gratitude has opened up my perspective on myself? My world?

_____

_____

_____

_____

Fostering Gratitude through Images

The abundantly positive experiences associated with gratitude mean that its power can be captured not just verbally but by engaging one's visual imagination. Accordingly, I asked a large number of people if they had an image or symbol that could convey what gratitude meant to them. Their images, described in their own words, are provided below. An added feature of many of these images is that they appear to convey not only the meaning of gratitude but also its positive outcome.

1. "The picture is a smiling face and two people hugging."
2. "Smile, God, praying hands. The symbols are of two hands praying, and a man rejoicing with his arms in the air."
3. "Unexpectedly receiving a present, a magic fairy that brings joy to people. The symbol is of a fairy touching a flower with her magic wand."
4. "Hiking in the mountains, and struggling to get to the top. When you reach the top, you are thankful for God creating such beauty. The symbol is one of a man standing on top of a mountain and viewing all the scenery around him."
5. "The symbol of a Thanksgiving basket."

6. "The symbols of red hearts and flowers."
7. "A person kneeling and praying, completely broken, and worshiping God. A child hugging a parent full of love and compassion."
8. "A bond between a mother and child that can't be broken."
9. "A full-length glass door that beckons me to pass through, not to repay but to engage and contribute to the practice of loving-kindness as unselfishly as I am able."
10. "Quietude, a garden or forest (trees and/or flowers) and a solitary figure in a receptive or contemplative state. It is sun-lit, but not glaring."
11. "A weary traveler being given food, drink, and rest."
12. "When I think of grateful, I see a bond that I formed, something that can't be broken."
13. "What I picture are small things that can happen, such as a person picking something up for someone else."
14. "Exclamation point."
15. "I usually think of a kid that unexpectedly receives a present. Or when you get a package unexpectedly in the mail."
16. "A smile."
17. "When you go on a hike in the mountains. The hike is a struggle but when you get to the end, the view is awesome."
18. "Sun-filled days or a hill with a warm breeze blowing, sitting in the middle of the road on a hill."
19. "The wild flowers in an open field symbolize for me the trust that motivates my feeling of being grateful."
20. "A mother riding on a subway while breast-feeding her new-born."
21. "Flowers—all flowers everywhere."
22. "Being held by God. I'm sitting on his lap with my head on his chest. He has his arms wrapped around me."

After reading the above list, respond to the following:

- Which two or three images above most appeal to you? What is it about each of these images that you find most attractive? Why?

- If you were asked to provide an apt symbol or image for gratitude, what would it be?
- Take a sheet of paper and draw your gratitude. Why this drawing? What features of your drawing are most significant for you?

Conclusion

To be aware of the power of gratitude, we need only quickly review gratitude's effects. From the discussion above, it appears that gratitude is associated with maturity, inspiration, insight, positive behaviors, positive emotions, human connection (dependency), awareness, fullness, and open-mindedness. Further, when people offer symbols for gratitude, their images are threaded with sensitivity, warmth, joy, and compassion. These positive features fit closely in line with psychologist Barbara Fredrickson's "broadening and building" theory of positive emotions.[42] According to Fredrickson, positive emotions such as joy, love, and gratitude broaden what we think and how we act. Positive emotions encourage us "to play, to explore, to envision future achievements, and to savor and integrate."[43] For example, with a pleasant emotion such as joy, we are apt to find ourselves more creative and engaged in life and flexible in the choices we make. At the same time, in addition to broadening how we might think and proceed, positive emotions have a "building" effect on our lives by expanding the resources available to us. For example, when happy, we are better able to cope. If we happen to encounter a stressful situation while in a joyful mood, our pleasant state will encourage effective coping strategies, such as eliminating the stress through problem solving, employing some countermeasure such as engaging in a hobby, or enlisting support by seeking out friends. In contrast to the broadening and building features of positive emotions, negative emotions lock us in to a limited range of thoughts and behaviors. If we are fearful, for instance, our thoughts are rigidly focused on the source of our fear and how we might get out of the situation and avoid similar encounters in the future.

The "broaden and build" aspects of gratitude are particularly noteworthy. According to Fredrickson, gratitude expands and creatively stretches people's thinking, allowing them to consider increasingly diverse ways in which they might help and benefit others. In addition, gratitude "builds" a wide variety of "goods" in people's lives. Gratitude, she observes, fosters friendships, strengthens people's bonds to the community, enhances spiritual practices, and promotes loving and caring responses to others.[44] In sum, as we review the "effects of gratitude," we can't help but conclude that these positive features broaden how we relate to the world and build up our lives in ways that benefit others.

Throughout this chapter, we have significantly expanded gratitude's scope. The first approach allows us to set boundaries for gratitude by examining the nature of ingratitude. Utilizing the second and third approaches has enabled us to view some of gratitude's complexity along with its basic link to everyday emotional experience. Finally, the fourth approach enables us to understand the seemingly endless positive benefits associated with gratitude's origins, as well as its consequences. In the next chapter we continue this exploration with a new twist: What do humans need to have if we are to live our lives gratefully?

Chapter Four

GROWING IN GRATITUDE

There I was—a hunk of brown drab clay.
No shape, no form, of no use.
Many came and tried to mold me
Into a useful shape so that
I could be used and enjoyed by all.
None was able to accomplish the task!
But then came one who knew what to do.
He worked, kneaded and trimmed and added, too.
Slowly, oh ever so slowly, the brown drab clay
Developed into a grace-filled vessel
From which living nature waters could flow.
—*Poem entitled "Gratitude" written*
by a woman in her sixty-sixth year

Many years ago, when starting out as a young therapist, I had a pivotal moment in my clinical training that taught me the healing power of gratitude. I was assigned as the therapist to a young adolescent whom I will call Ashley. She suffered from numerous losses and traumas, including the sudden deaths of loved ones and sexual abuse. As a beginning therapist I tried to do all the "right" things. I treated her with great respect in order to strengthen her sense of boundaries, which some adults in her past had ignored. I empathized with her and gave soothing feedback to the numerous accounts she shared with me about her life. Attempting to be sensitive to her fragile psychological state, I inquired about her many traumas carefully and cautiously and let her take the lead, again to demonstrate to her that I could be a reliably trusted adult, unlike the many adults who had abandoned or hurt her. Above all, I wanted to convey to her that she could feel safe with me as we explored the many hurts she had already suffered.

One day while walking through the hospital ward, I was reflecting on our sessions together. It occurred to me that our therapy sessions had overwhelmingly focused on negative events—emotional hurts and traumas that had been inflicted on her. As such, I just felt that something was missing in our interactions. I feared that when she left the hospital she would be without anything, from a psychological perspective, to call her own. In other words, Ashley had no psychological "turf" to ground her and on which she could draw. I reasoned, without trying to be naive or simplistic, that her therapy had to be more than just working through painful emotions and traumatic memories. Though dealing with emotional wounds and scars is central to the therapeutic process, I wondered if there was some positive "active ingredient" I could introduce into our sessions that Ashley could seize upon and embrace; something that would stay with her and affirm her for who she was. As I thought about what this ingredient might be, the question "What is she grateful for?" came to mind. Upon further reflection, I felt it worth the gamble to introduce the topic of gratitude into our therapy discussions. At our next session, at a strategic point when we both sat in comfortable silence, I decided to take the plunge. I began cautiously with, "Ashley, we have talked about a number of painful things and we still need to talk about them more, but I'd like to switch gears for a moment and ask you something: Is there anything you are grateful for?" She responded quizzically to my unanticipated question. I gently rephrased the question and tried again: "We've talked about many things that have been hurtful, and I know I'm shifting the discussion, but I was just wondering what you might appreciate about your life or are thankful for?" Though hesitant at first, she spoke concretely about a letter she had received from a friend. This response sparked a brief discussion about the value of friendship and how it is important to be grateful for friends. With encouragement, she mentioned several other things that I can no longer remember. As therapy progressed over the next few months until her discharge, we attempted in every session to spend a few moments focusing on why she could feel grateful.

I sincerely believe that this turn of events aided Ashley's healing. By focusing on gratitude, she was able to discover a healing psychological turf on which to stand. She had, in other words, a conscious experience of *gift* in her life. As therapy progressed, this became an increasingly powerful antidote for breaking up her never-ending loops of negative thinking or for tempering and containing intensely felt reactions of hurt and anger, which before had all too easily spiraled out of control. Abuse victims frequently are imprisoned by self-hatred. They frequently come to view themselves as bad and struggle with enormous feelings of shame. As I reflect back on our time together, I have come to see that Ashley's gratitude had been a soothing balm. Discussions of gratitude helped her to feel "gifted" (though we never used that word) and made her aware of a sense of her own goodness that began to provide a refreshing and liberating positive alternative to the troubling moods and negative thoughts that made up so much of her daily life.

Ever since my time with Ashley, as a psychologist I have placed a high premium on having clients be conscious of gratitude in their lives. In working with numerous clients over the past few decades, I have more or less concluded that a client's capacity for healing is proportional to his or her ability to feel and grow in gratitude.

The Capacity for Gratitude

Fortunately, Ashley possessed the capacity both to recognize her gratitude and to grow in it. If we are to become people of gratitude, then obviously we must nurture the qualities necessary for its expression. And so we need to consider: *What personal qualities do we need if we are to grow in gratitude?* Below are listed some essential features we need to address if we wish to live a grateful life. As we discuss each one, reflect on the degree to which each is a vital element in your own life.

OTHER POSITIVE EMOTIONS

As we have already seen, a number of emotions cluster around gratitude. People expressed feelings such as joy, hope, and love. One may well wonder whether gratitude creates other positive feelings; whether other positive emotions lead to gratitude; or whether a third factor, such as having grown up in a household in which one was exposed to numerous affirming experiences, generates both gratitude and other positive feelings. The precise nature of the relationship between gratitude and other positive feelings need not concern us; what's important is to recognize that the association does exist, since gratitude is a positive emotion and pleasantly felt emotions do cluster together. If we desire a grateful heart, then we need to cultivate in our lives other emotions such as the warmth of love, the delight of surprise, and the trust that comes with hope.

THE EXPERIENCE OF EMPATHY

Gratitude requires that we be sensitively attuned to another's intentions. In general terms, empathy can be defined as being able to understand another's perspective while simultaneously experiencing his or her joys and sorrows as if they are our own. Through empathy we come to discern another's goodness and its effects on us. If we are to have gratitude toward another, we have to perceive that their actions toward us lead to a positive effect and that their action benefits us in some way. In short, from the perspective of gratitude, empathy serves as a key to help us unlock the power of goodness through accurately perceiving another's intentions.

A wonderful description of gratitude is depicted by a character in Scott Turow's novel *Personal Injuries*. Robbie, a poignantly flawed attorney, starts up a conversation describing how he got to know his law partner, Morty. When Robbie was a child, his father had abandoned him. As a result, in order to feed the family, his mother went to work, leaving six-year-old Robbie with a neighbor and her chronically sick son, Morty. At first, Morty is the object of his disdain. Robbie detested Morty's infirmities. For six months, he would slap him around until one day it dawned on him that Morty felt bad too, that everyone has a hurt, that everyone has pain somewhere inside them. Whether it's a matter of being poor or sick or alone, or of feeling unloved or inadequate, hurt is inescapable. Robbie wondered why God would create a world in which everyone's heart is in pain. The answer came to him that it was so that we would need one another, stick together, and not simply go off on our own.[1]

What is revealing about this conversation? For one, it is a beautiful story of empathy as Robbie comes to understand and appreciate Morty's humanness. Second, it is a comment on gratitude. Throughout the passage, the theme of gratitude is clear though implicit. Robbie learns to appreciate Morty as a gift he was given. It is not overstated to say that without empathy, gratitude has no chance.

This incident from Turow's novel provides us a second critical reason why empathy is important for gratitude. Besides helping us to understand another, empathy is the catalyst for acting in the world or, in the context of gratitude, it triggers in us the sympathy to then act compassionately in the world—to give away the goodness that we have received. In the case of Robbie and Morty, they lived a friendship based on mutual loyalty and care.

THE GROWTH OF IDENTITY

Identity is the receptacle of gratitude. We increasingly acquire our identity as we address the question: Who am I? Among other things, identity originates from the myriad people, events, and cultural influences that shape our lives. Influential people sustain us, specific events define us, and cultural influences shape us. The latter are strong: contrast the attitudes toward money, financial concerns, and the work of people whose formative years were shaped by the Great Depression and those of Generations X and Y, or, with the most recent entry in generational shifts, the Millennials!

Identity is both stable and changing. No matter what our age we know we are the same person as when we were eight—yet, we are also aware, as we look back, that we have changed. Old but new, constant yet changing, identity conveys the way we understand ourselves even as we continue to "explain" ourselves to others through our actions, attitudes, and perceptions.[2] Identity provides the necessary inner coherence that forges our sense of continuity. Thus, identity serves as the vehicle to guide the evolving story we construct over the years, providing it both meaning and purpose.

One other point worth noting: for the most part, identity is incomplete until the last stages of life. Though we most certainly can describe ourselves at thirty-five more adequately than when we were fifteen, there still remains much that can happen to and influence who we are. So many possibilities, some anticipated and others not, can intrude into our futures. A parent dies, a new relationship is formed, we uproot and move, a friend betrays us, a once-sacred belief is altered, or a cause we deeply commit ourselves to proves initially liberating though eventually disappointing. All these events and so many more help to mold a stable yet evolving self-definition. As our lives continue to unfold, we select those meaningful life themes that permit us to articulate the sense of who we are and how we wish to present ourselves to others. With regard to gratitude specifically, continuity with our past helps us to grow more aware of the accumulated kindnesses that have been shown us. Over time, we come increasingly to value gratefulness and place more importance on representing this truth to others as it weaves itself into our self-definitions. Valuing it and the benefits it brings so highly, we seek further opportunities to express it. Over time, we come to recognize gratitude as an enduring life theme. As identity more incorporates gratitude, it grows into an essential ingredient of who we are. Thus, a deeply grateful person who is asked to define who he or she is can assert confidently that one defining quality is, simply, "I *am* grateful."

In one touching example of this growth process, a college graduate shared with me how he and his younger brother had continually fought during their teen years. Recently he received a package from his younger sibling. It contained a small, inexpensive, but, for the student who was sharing this story, highly personal gift. The student told me it was one of the best gifts he had ever received; it signified to him how he and his brother were now growing closer. The rivalry was subsiding. The two of them are doing things together that in previous years seemed unimaginable. They had now come to the point where competition yielded to appreciation. What allowed this to occur was each growing increasingly comfortable with who he himself was. Gradually shedding their rivalry as the source of their identity building, and replacing it with a newly acquired appreciation for the other, they could bond in a way that only several years ago seemed inconceivable. In the process, each could begin to appreciate the other in a new way. Thus, one brother shows his own growing contentment with himself by sending his brother a special gift. The older brother could accept it more easily because of his own personal growth. He told me he subsequently looked forward to being with his younger brother and "doing things together," which can certainly be interpreted as giving back a gift. I suspect the seeds are being planted for a future life theme of brotherly appreciation (mutual gift-giving). In the years ahead they are apt to see each other more and more as the "gift given me" and, when reflecting on their relationship, experience gratitude for it.

A MEMORY OF GRATITUDE

If identity is the receptacle of gratitude, then memory is its nourishment. Traveling the journey to greater gratitude involves having life stories that contain such memories. Too often, however, these are lost, ignored, or taken for granted. As one commentator observes, "We are basket cases of ingratitude, so many of us."[3] Moreover,

> we cannot hope to repay in kind what Socrates gave us, but to live without any sense of obligation to those who made possible lives as tolerable as ours, within the frame of the human predicament God imposed on us—without any sense of gratitude to our parents, who suffered to raise us; to our teachers, who labored to teach us; to the scientists, who prolonged the lives of our children when disease struck them down—is spiritually atrophying.[4]

Without memory, gratitude evaporates. When thankful memories surface, recollections of people, situations, and experiences nurture grateful outlooks. It is as if one possessed a database in which calling up many acts of gratefulness becomes routine. The great humanitarian and Nobel laureate Elie Wiesel has pointed out that memories can be rich sources of gratitude for both young and old. Commenting on the roots of Jewish tradition, he notes that it has long celebrated the elderly, and he suggests that "to honor an old person, as we are commanded to do in scripture, is a way of showing gratitude."[5] Older adults provide us with the lessons of history, informing and passing on their knowledge and insights. The elderly, in turn, find their gratitude resting in a huge repository of previously lived grateful "moments turned memories" where this storehouse initiates its own gift-giving, still. An excellent example of the grateful dedication of older Americans resides in the innumerable ways grandparents stand by and support both their adult children and grandchildren. If grandparents were to vanish, the social bonds and emotional fabrics of countless families would turn chaotic and unravel.

The content that makes up memories of gratitude takes many forms. For nearly all of us, this storage of numerous memories contains highly personalized and cherished relationships that evoke the stirrings of gratitude. These are the significant people threaded through our lives whose love made a difference. They frequently include the parents who cared for us, the siblings who were our companions during our early journeys, the authority figures (such as teachers and coaches) who offered us guidance along the way, and the steadfast friends who stood by us in times of need. When stepping back to scan their past, most people are often struck by the sheer number of people whose influence has shaped them.

A marvelous and true relationship that movingly captures "a memory of gratitude" is sportswriter Mitch Albom's inspiring recollections of the final days of Morrie Schwartz, his college professor at Brandeis University. Morrie had been the single most significant influence throughout Mitch's undergraduate years, and at graduation he pledged, as do so many of us, to fulfill the now ritualized and well-worn promise to "stay in touch." Like most of us, the dreams and demands of young adulthood distracted him from fulfilling his promise. He did indeed think about Morrie now and then and the things Morrie had taught him about being human and relating to others, but it always seemed to have come from another life.[6] Many years later, now a successful sportswriter in Detroit, Mitch finds himself flipping channels and comes upon a news show featuring his frail yet still-beloved professor. The theme of the broadcast is Morrie's health—he is slowly dying from amyotrophic lateral sclerosis (ALS, commonly known as Lou Gehrig's disease). Jarred by past personal memories, Mitch contacts his old mentor and promises to visit him. Completing his journey in anxious anticipation, the student is once again reunited with his teacher and the sportswriter willingly takes on the task (or, as Mitch might well describe it, the "honor") of chronicling Tuesday meetings with his old instructor.

One cannot read this short, eloquently written book without admiring Morrie. He lived his last year with dignity, teaching others how to love and find meaning even while slowly being strangled by a hideous neurological disease. What Mitch depicts in this enriching book is the enduringly loving nature of Morrie's integrity as lived out through unwavering loyal bonds to his former student, his family, his

friends, and his community, even as he approached the fated certainty of his own death. Morrie's willingness to speak openly about
his ultimate demise becomes, through their Tuesday encounters, the
teacher and student's "last class" together. Though the focus of the
book is on Morrie Schwartz's humble and seasoned wisdom, I can't
help but be struck by another significant point: the book is a fitting
testament to the power of gratitude. During those precious Tuesday
conversations, the author voices an appreciation whose depth pervades every turn of the page. In the final, brief concluding chapter,
Mitch Albom observes rightly that no one can undo what they have
done, or relive his or her life; but if Morrie had taught him anything,
it was that there is no such thing in life as "too late": until the day
he died, Morrie never stopped changing.[7] Mitch then writes about
his newly found need to reach out to rekindle the relationship with
his brother and tell him, "I don't want to lose you. I love you."[8] Even
in death, the old professor (whom Mitch fondly called "coach") was
still teaching. And Mitch, his ardent student, was eagerly still learning how to give away the gift he experienced from Morrie, as seen in
his concern for his own brother.

   As time has afforded me the opportunity to reflect more on this
engrossing book, I have come to discover one of its most significant
points: an outflowing of gratitude that is threefold. First, there is the
ever-grateful professor who refuses to give up teaching all of us how to
be grateful. Second, there is his grateful pupil, Mitch, who captivates us
by his sensitive portrayal of this wise man. Finally, there are the rest of
us, who can't help but be grateful for Morrie and Mitch's collaborative
relationship, making it a font of instructive, timeless wisdom for all.

   In addition to the highly personal relationships that trigger so
many fond memories of gratitude, we can also be touched by more
broadened memories contained in our cultural histories. One woman
whom I interviewed movingly described her trip to Pearl Harbor and
the memorial to the battleship Arizona. She remembered reflecting on
how "you are who you are because of who came before you." Similarly,
observances of Memorial Day or Independence Day, or a visit to the
tomb of the unknown soldier, may evoke historical gratitude.

   Moreover, gratitude frequently appears in the speeches of
national leaders both as a way to communicate personal feelings and
as a way to unite the country in times of trial. Speaking at the

Democratic National Convention as his second term drew to a close, President Clinton told his audience: "Fifty-four years ago this week, I was born in a summer storm to a young widow in a small southern town. America gave me the chance to live my dreams. I have tried to give you a better chance to live yours. Now, with hair graying and wrinkles deeper, but with the same optimism and hope I brought to the work I loved eight years ago, my heart is filled with gratitude."[9] And after the tragic events of September 11, President Bush echoed the thoughts of so many Americans when he noted: "We are thankful for new heroes—police officers and firefighters and emergency workers, who have renewed our respect for public service and provided lasting lessons in courage."[10] The most recent presidential election also evidenced gratitude themes. Senator John McCain frequently expressed the gratitude he felt at being able to serve his country through both military life and public service. Similarly, then Senator Barack Obama often expressed his gratitude for the opportunities America had provided, given his humble beginnings. Truly, memories of gratitude are both personal and public.

A CONSCIOUSNESS OF GRATITUDE

For our gratitude to deepen, our awareness of gratitude must be a conscious, everyday decision. As Charles Dickens once remarked, "Reflect on your present blessings, of which every man has many, not on your past misfortunes, of which all have some."[11] Obviously, knowing one has gratitude does not mean we are consciously attuned to it at every waking moment. Daily hassles, moments of stress, and unforeseen crises all too readily evoke negative feelings or shift our focus, thus eclipsing any conscious sense of gratitude. Quite simply, it takes continual motivation and effort to keep gratitude conscious. What a consciousness of gratitude offers is a reliable lens through which to experience, not only the presence of gratitude, but also its consequences as well. The consciousness we develop sensitizes us to perceive our gifted state in the many people, innumerable events, and unpredictable situations we encounter daily. Obviously, the more that gratitude roots itself within us, the more apt we are to perceive life gratefully.[12] Additionally, having grateful awareness awakens us to gratitude's surprise.

What must be emphasized is the need to *cultivate* gratitude. Desirable habits take practice! One of the delights of gratitude is the simple fact that we can create it at almost any opportunity. We must remember continually to select from our daily lives all for which we are grateful, and to take the time to explore how gratitude encircles so much of what we do and who we are. Indifference subverts our gratitude. Apathy toward life undermines the awareness required to live gratefully. We must counter this by making a point of savoring all of life's gifts, in all their innumerable forms. For example, one person maintains his gratitude-awareness by enjoying frequent recollections of his family, listening to classical music, taking trips to the mountains, and periodically rewarding himself by a good meal out. Diversity helps gratitude. We must make the effort to expand the daily sources of our gratitude. Pause for a moment to consider: how do you cultivate gratitude on a daily basis?

Additionally, gratitude is a *choice* we make. Remember, we can literally produce gratitude at almost any moment of our lives! This is part of the appeal of gratitude. As we have seen, sometimes stressful events burden us or painful memories blind us, thereby preventing us from recognizing our blessings. Yet, even in the midst of such distress, we can frequently refocus (though admittedly with great effort) on other events and choose a recollection for triggering gratitude, thereby offering an alternative to stagnating in self-pity or sulking in negative feelings. Opting to live gratefully is to some degree nearly always possible.

Our consciousness of gratitude leads us down a trail that is *hope-filled*. Living with a hopeful sense does not require that we enjoy great success or that we always view the future with unbounded optimism. What it does lead to is a growing and unshakable belief, based on our current awareness of gratitude, that some goodness is always possible and that we ourselves can emerge as sources for bringing it about.

A LIFE PERSPECTIVE

It is only with age that our life perspective grows. With regard to gratitude, a life perspective means, first, becoming increasingly aware of our insufficiency and, secondly, realizing that life could have been otherwise. Discerning our insufficiency surfaces from several sources. First, as we continue into our adult years, we are increasingly confronted with the fact that our lives have borne loss, disappointment, and failure. Not all of our dreams have come true and no doubt some, if not many, remain unfulfilled or, in retrospect, are now acknowledged as having been unrealistic. Yet we can balance this realization with the many positive events we have experienced, and most of us are able to fashion a life story where the positive aspects triumph or at least are not overwhelmed by unrealized hopes. Also, as the years go by, we increasingly learn of the misfortunes of so many. Quite naturally, this leads to comparisons with our own more fortunate situation. Frequently, the first serious realization of this seeming imbalance occurs in adolescence. For example, several times I have heard adolescents and young adults talk about times when they were on a retreat with peers, during which they participated in group sharing sessions. One young person had the typical adolescent strains and tensions with his parents but shared that he now began to view his relationship with them in a new light. While participating in a group, he was amazed to hear the truly awful situations some of his peers spoke about. Such newly acquired knowledge caused him to reassess his relationship with his parents and appreciate them more.

In addition, we can vicariously live other people's disadvantaged states. Simply because of the mere fact of living longer, we are more exposed to the tragedies and heartaches of those we know in person, with many of whom we have emotional and meaningful ties. The more emotional ties we share, the more exposed we are to others' plights. Further, the deeper our emotional bonds with certain persons, the more apt we are to be affected by their adversity, and inevitably we will compare their unfortunate state to our own. More often than not, such comparisons create some sense of gratitude for our own more fortunate circumstances. We are, for example, grateful for loved ones who remain alive, for the health we have, for the success that has come our way, and for all the times we have been able to avoid accidents. But we realize that things could have been otherwise. Accordingly, as we enter our middle and later years, our exposure to so much misfortune, as well as the misfortune we ourselves have endured, leads us to view life as fragile. We come increasingly to realize the frailty of life, and how what we enjoy at the moment could so easily be lost or gone tomorrow. All in all, gratitude seems to be the only sensible response.

A WELL-FUNCTIONING CONSCIENCE

A life of deepening gratitude requires that we commit ourselves to goodness; only people of integrity live truly good lives. Only conscience can ensure that we are women and men of integrity. Conscience is a uniquely human quality that requires us to make choices that reflect goodness, to follow through on our choices, and to commit ourselves to the choices we make.[13] Gratitude is linked to conscience just by the fact that we could never acknowledge, live out, or give back our giftedness unless we had within us some prior moral sense that recognizes the gracious generosity of giving and motivates us to give back in turn for what we have received.

A HUMBLE STANCE

Gratitude of any depth goes hand in hand with humility. Humility does not mean that we disregard who we are; rather, it means that we accept our talents (and thereby maximize our ability to be gift-givers) along with our limitations (and thereby acknowledge our dependence on others). Humility enables us to accept those limitations we cannot alter while patiently attending to those limitations that can be improved.[14] Humility also surrenders to dependence. Even the most minimal expression of appreciation—saying, "Thank-you"—entails the recognition of our dependence upon another, even if the situation is quite temporary (e.g., a stranger takes a second to hold the door for someone else). Further, the acceptance of talents or limitations always requires that we affirm another's helping hand. To grow in gratitude we must accept that acknowledging our dependencies, rather than viewing them as burdens, is necessary if we are to live a full and satisfying life.

THE CAPACITY FOR REDEMPTION

Inevitably, negative events can sometimes bring wounds and leave scars that may endure for life. At the same time, however, gratitude can be both the process for finding redemption in such moments and the prize achieved when doing so. This was highlighted for me by one person's poignant story about a childhood experience in which he ran through a muddy field and unthinkingly entered his house and muddied the kitchen floor. He bore his mother's scolding and the humiliation of being slapped in the face. The painful sting of this event stayed with him through the years. Several decades later, a small group of middle-aged African Americans shared their childhood stories with him. Being the first black students to attend newly desegregated, all-white schools, they were surrounded by an unruly white crowd and pelted with mud and rocks as they emerged from the school bus. When they entered the school with their clothes now soiled, they were rebuked by their teachers for their appearance! My friend said that the story told by these African Americans led him to recall the incident with his mother. He found himself feeling strangely grateful for the scolding he had received, because it helped him to understand more fully the pain and injustice experienced by African Americans. Thus, what had been a cause of shame was now transformed into a newly felt bond toward others that subsequently renewed his commitment to addressing issues of social injustice through his current job.

In the above story we see elements of several features that make up the capacity for gratitude. There is empathy for African Americans, along with a life perspective that allows him to see misfortune as he compares his own life with theirs. Even so, the redemptive focus for this story is paramount: it is the capacity for redemption that makes the very experience endurable and insight-provoking. The possibility of gratitude fuels the redemption process along. This conversion of pain to redemption offers him hope that other negative memories might also become instructive and even inspiring. Consequently, this redemptive process affords healing. Furthermore, it provides a purpose for the future by offering a perspective to engage the world with hope-filled endeavors; that is, if the past can be redeemed, we can more readily embrace a world in which pain exists, for, having already savored the benefits of redemption, we are left with a new reassurance that we can engage the world, whatever it might hold.

This redemptive capacity is most responsible for the human ability to acquire gratitude from virtually any experience. For example, Adam, a psychotherapy client of mine for several years, had suffered from a lingering depression for several decades. He had tried numerous antidepressant medications but to no avail. Nothing seemed able to shake the depressive symptoms that dogged him. These included difficulty sleeping, lack of motivation, and a general malaise and listlessness that seemed to color most of what he did. Fortunately, he was able to put on a good front with most people, but daily life was in many ways a struggle. I vividly remember the day when Adam said to me, "You know, when all is said and done, I'm really glad I'm depressed." He elaborated further: "Well, as you know, I've been struggling with this depression for several years and I just can't seem to shake it. What is interesting is that neither of my two brothers, or my sister, or my parents have it, just me. And I was thinking the other day, if someone had to have it in my family, I'm glad it was me because I just wouldn't want any of my siblings or parents to have it. I for sure don't want it but if someone in my family has to have it, I'm glad it's me because I wouldn't want them to go through this." As Adam's therapist, I was humbled. I knew him to be an honest person who loved his parents and siblings deeply. His response was a simple, heartfelt expression of gracious generosity. He was redeeming his struggle. The gratitude he felt in his struggle with depression gave hope and meaning to his life. Though admittedly at times we might have to look long and hard for the gratitude moment in some of our experiences, it is usually there in some way, and we are then open to being empowered for some noble purpose.

SOLITUDE

As we have already seen, the human tendency to take one's blessings for granted represents one of the most significant stumbling blocks to gratitude. We need to devote the time necessary for reflecting on our many gifts. For example, our relationship with someone significant in our life can be enhanced only if we periodically take the time to reflect on the meaning, the health, and the future of the relationship. Any belief we cherish benefits from time spent reflecting on it more deeply and, ideally, examining it more critically. Thus, one essential quality required for us to grow in gratitude is setting aside time for reflection. Building on the above, when we redirect our focus and *consciously* use the theme of "gift" as our guide, most often we are flooded with greater awareness of the gifts we do have. A place where we lived, a person who helped us, the health or infirmity we had, an insight gained, a surprise that mattered, a sorrow that opened our eyes, a success we savored, a defeat we learned from, a troublesome behavior successfully addressed—all such occasions become possibilities for our gratitude when we give them the necessary focus that only solitude allows. Solitude offers the opportunity for insightful and thought-provoking reflection through which we discover the generosity we have experienced along with the generosity we can give.

A Checklist for Growing in Gratitude

How might we measure our ability to grow in gratitude? The capacities needed for gratitude offer us a guide. Simply go through the following questions and assess your motivation (how deeply you desire) to respond positively to each.

Positive Emotions: Which people, thoughts, and events contribute most to my enjoyment of life?

Empathy: When interacting with others, what priority do I give to understanding them and responding to them with compassion?

Identity: Do I like the challenge of getting to know myself better and discovering new things about myself?

Memory: How enthused am I with making a conscious effort to remember the good things that have happened to me?

Consciousness: Am I willing to make the resolve on a daily basis to remember things in my life that I am grateful for?

Life Perspective: Do I desire to grow in the ability to recognize that the frailty of life calls me to admit that many things in my life could have been otherwise and to be grateful for who I am and what I have, no matter how much or how little it might be?

Conscience: Do I desire to make my good life better? Accordingly, will I do whatever I need to in order to foster a life of integrity?

Humility: In the years ahead, do I wish to live humbly? Am I comfortable with knowing that my life is significant, while at the same time knowing how much I rely on others and have to learn from them?

Redemption: Do I believe that the pains and struggles in my life can also be opportunities for growth in, and insight about, myself?

Solitude: Am I committed to finding time to reflect on the gratitude I have?

To the degree to which we respond affirmatively to these questions and engage them with willing enthusiasm in the years ahead, to
that degree we will grow in gratitude.

The Development of Gratitude

Some emotions are basic and appear to be present at or within
several months of birth. We speak without hesitation of a toddler
being frightened or happy, but we would refrain from describing a
two-year-old as "grateful." Psychiatrist Edmund Bergler notes that
gratitude gets off to "a bad start" because in the first few years of a
child's life, his or her assumptions about the attention, food, and care
received is simply assumed to be rightfully his or hers and is taken for
granted.[15] Over time what transpires is the child's gradual shedding of
this narrow perspective and growing recognition that other people
possess distinct thoughts and feelings that differ from his or her own.
Yet even these early years of childhood, commonly seen as a time of
great self-absorption, are not what they seem. Psychologists now
know that even children as young as two are capable of acts of kindness and generosity, thus defying the commonly held assumption that
selfishness is the sole driving force in the toddler's life.[16]

Generally speaking, the seeds of gratitude are planted in these
early years, assuming that the child receives nurturing care. A child's
gratitude has its roots in a nourishing family environment. Early on,
parents encourage children to acquire language routines. Acting
politely and saying thank-you are two behaviors strongly reinforced
by parents during these formative years.[17] Added to this ongoing
instruction is the child's continuing growth, such that "with increasing age, children appear to acquire a good deal of insight into emotional processes."[18] This developing insight is readily seen in the
child's understanding of his or her own experience of gratitude. Thus,
at ages four or five, children know that gratitude "feels good" but
they are unable to comprehend fully the situations that require them
to express gratitude. Older children and adolescents, on the other
hand, more accurately assess what situations should warrant them to
respond gratefully. As children develop, it is likely that complex
emotions such as gratitude exert more influence on their behavior,

and over time children accurately perceive situations that call them to express gratitude. They tell themselves that they should feel grateful and their grateful feelings in turn lead them to behave gratefully.[19] Most certainly, by early adolescence (age twelve) the child possesses the intellectual skills necessary for interpreting accurately when someone has responded freely and generously in a way that deserves a grateful response.[20]

"Common sense and personal experience suggest that the quality of family life and sibling relationships, the effects of peers and the media, the influence of schools and churches and the overall level of civility that characterizes a child's social world all play some role in the development of gratitude."[21] The spillover effects of these many influences are most certainly seen in the teen years. Adolescents and young adults are capable of gratitude; the quality of this gratitude begins to differ from that of childhood years and in some cases it can be felt profoundly. The teen years usher in a more sophisticated sense of self-understanding, along with a greater capacity to think in complex and critical ways.[22] Young people sort out and make sense of their worlds by their newly acquired abilities to think in abstract terms, to understand their own and others' life histories, to consider the unique circumstances of people in diverse social situations, to dream possibilities, and to struggle and reconcile with the realities before them. It stands to reason that the changes they undergo allow their gratitude to take on a different quality. As the psychologist Dan McAdams notes, "Whereas the 7-year old can thank a teacher for showing her how to write her name, the 17-year old can feel gratitude for a teacher's showing her how to live a good life."[23]

The most fertile area for youth's experience of gratitude is through relationships. If we had to define the essence of youth, it would be existing "in relationship." It is through relationships that adolescents best acquire identity, come to know themselves, and negotiate their journey to adulthood. Young people are in a continual process of redefining relationships with parents and other authority figures. They seek solace and security in peer groups, while at the same time fashioning their own unique perspective on the world. They engage themselves, at times intensely so, in friendships and romantic attachments. At any one point in a teen or young adult's life, relationships wax and wane and are in various stages of intensifying, complexifying, or disintegrating. The adjustments required by ever-evolving relationships lead adolescents to self-discovery. More and more they grow in insights regarding themselves, their world, other people: how they have arrived at this moment, what could have been different, and what the future might hold. In all of these experiences and moments they have the opportunity to find gratitude.

Yet, though the depth of youth's gratitude is more pronounced than that of their childhood years, their gratitude still lacks the qualities that arise (but are in no way guaranteed) by the middle and later adult years. The most likely reason for this is, simply, that the typical high school and college-age young people still lack an adequate life perspective for genuine gratitude. The possibilities, opportunities, and choices that characterize the middle adult years are yet to be experienced by youth. As a consequence, their outlook on their own lives as well as on the world is, for the most part, limiting. Most have yet to struggle significantly with opportunities for what might have been, endure the disappointments and sobering reality of faded dreams, or wrestle with the complexities of important decisions, and they have not lived long enough to be able to look back on earlier years and come to a sense of peace. One college professor who has taught young adults for over two decades summarized this fact when he said that "college students can certainly be grateful and I have witnessed it over the years. But by and large they can't be 'really' grateful for the simple reason that they don't have enough years behind them. And to put it bluntly, if they don't have enough years, then they don't know the disappointments and heartaches those added years bring—and all of these experiences are necessary for true gratitude." Only with advancing age and the experiences it holds will the roots of gratitude reach more deeply.

The Reality of Distorted Gratitude

Before we move on to the final chapter in which we come to understand the fullest meaning and expression of gratitude, we need to consider one final topic. As the last few chapters have shown, the positive features of gratitude are numerous, yet this abundance of favorable features can prove seductive. On the one hand, the potential for emotional, physical, spiritual, and moral health that gratitude offers is incontestable. On the other hand, we want to avoid the trap of viewing this valued emotion uncritically and superficially. It is fair to say that the favorable light in which some writers on spirituality have regarded gratitude has been both excessive and naive.[24]

Why spend time on the topic of distorted gratitude? Besides the needed corrective to the overly positive evaluation that gratitude has received in some circles, one further reason stands out. The lack of a critical discussion of gratitude renders the very notion of gratitude as a moral emotion questionable. A now generally accepted notion in both psychology and ethics is the presence of "moral emotions," of which gratitude is one. In a general sense, an emotion is labeled moral if its presence elicits behavior that expresses concern for others and improvement of the human condition. Yet, don't most tyrants, criminals, and those who might wish us ill have some sincere capacity for gratitude that their actions are beneficial, at least to some? Most certainly. Unless we can identify distortions of gratitude, then gratitude itself remains suspect and risks contamination as we are unable to view it in an unqualified moral sense.

Consider the following question: Was Hitler capable of gratitude? Such a question proves unsettling. Who among us is inclined to respond with an unqualified "yes"? For most people, Hitler represents the personification of the twentieth-century's yielding to evil.[25] Even so, Hitler was a human being and, barring severe neurological or intellectual impairment, human beings are capable of experiencing gratitude. Nonetheless, the common conception of gratitude calls, viscerally, for an outright rejection of the notion that people like Hitler could be grateful. Still, the experience of gratitude is so pervasive in the human life cycle that to deny that even someone like Hitler experienced some level of gratefulness strains credulity. After all, this tyrant used the highly personal and intimate *du* form with some individuals (the German language distinguishes between two forms of the word *you*: the very intimate *du* and the more formal *sie*). Recent scholarship shows, moreover, that Hitler suffered from almost unbearable grief at the death of his mother.[26] Certainly such evidence is suggestive of some degree of gratefulness. Most certainly he was thankful for his Aryan lineage. Without question he had to consider that his ideas were useless unless he had loyal generals and troops to do his bidding, not to mention the sycophants surrounding him and the cadres of Nazi Party officials who carried out his perverted wishes. And then there were millions of Germans who were thankful that they had been given a leader who rectified the gross injustices of the Versailles Treaty and restored economic stability to the financially hapless German government.

Yet we need not confine ourselves to political tyrants. Were not the terrorists who forever changed America on September 11, 2001, capable of gratitude? Is it not reasonable to imagine them chanting prayers of gratitude for the success of their mission moments before the plane's fiery plunge into the side of the World Trade Center? Are we not to say that they were grateful? Moreover, political extremists, whether from the left or the right, express thanks when their twisted goals are achieved and their wishes carried out.

As a way of summary, how do we make sense of the gratitude that originates from injurious actions, ranging from the minor to those truly heinous? When we ponder these questions we come to view gratitude as somehow tainted.

As a way to address this dilemma, we must first acknowledge that the distorted forms of gratitude noted above are valid feelings of appreciation. But does appreciating the success of doing something wrong (e.g., stealing or killing) constitute true gratitude? *The answer to this question resides in the connection between gratitude and goodness.* Throughout these pages we have stressed gratitude's association with, among other things, the gift of goodness. From numerous interviews, individuals over and over speak about the power of gratitude experienced through a sense of being gifted through both the kindnesses they have received and subsequent kindnesses they return. In this resides gratitude's moral core. In other words, *true gratitude always bonds itself with goodness*, becoming in the process gratitude's *moral anchor*. Without goodness, authentic gratitude ceases to exist.

But what about common situations that don't appear to violate a moral principle? For example, if I place a dollar in a slot machine and after pulling the lever find myself with a win of $500, can I feel grateful for having played this particular slot machine? If my desire on a Saturday evening is to be with friends enjoying a football game rather than be at a formal reception where I am an award recipient, and I reluctantly attend the reception where I publicly express my thanks for the honor, do I qualify as a grateful person?

I believe the optimum way to address these concerns is to classify all experiences of appreciative sense that lack any connection with goodness as, more fittingly, one or another variation of distorted gratitude.

Distorted gratitude can be divided into quasi-gratitude (when questions of goodness appear negligible or absent) and harmful gratitude (when goodness is corrupted by hurtful behaviors). In order both to bring clarity to the discussion and to examine the complexity of distorted gratitude, I have identified seven types of quasi-gratitude and three types of harmful gratitude. The charts on the following pages provide a concise overview of distorted gratitude.

QUASI-GRATITUDE

Quasi-gratitude is unavoidable and exists as part and parcel of everyday life. There exist seven types of quasi-gratitude: (1) shallow gratitude, (2) reluctant gratitude, (3) self-serving gratitude, (4) defensive gratitude, (5) mixed gratitude, (6) misperceived gratitude, and (7) misplaced gratitude.

1. Shallow gratitude occurs when our thanks to others results from public pressure. When we express gratitude to satisfy audience expectations or in order to shield ourselves from resentment or ill will that would occur if we thanked no one, then our gratitude is shallow. A variation of this type might appear if we try to thank too many people, thereby diluting our thankfulness to those who truly matter.

2. If someone does us a kindness (e.g., mows our lawn), we feel the need to voice our thanks and show some kindness in return. But what if we would have rather mowed our own lawn and not be indebted to another for his or her kindness? In a sense, gratitude has trapped us! In such instances, our gratitude is clearly only reluctantly shown.

3. Sometimes people communicate thanks with an underlying motive of obtaining special favor or benefit. To illustrate, we might express our appreciation to our boss as a way to curry favor with him or her. Though not necessarily wrong, since

SEVEN TYPES OF QUASI-GRATITUDE

	MORAL QUALITY	TYPES	DEFINITION
QUASI-GRATITUDE	Quasi-gratitude depends on situations and intentions that usually point neither strongly toward nor strongly away from the good. For the most part, quasi-gratitude is perhaps best defined as morally neutral.	1. Shallow	Gratitude that is influenced by public pressure
		2. Reluctant	Gratitude that is forced upon us
		3. Self-Serving	Gratitude that is employed to obtain a desired outcome
		4. Defensive	Gratitude that is used to conceal unpleasant emotions
		5. Mixed	Gratitude that contains both positive and negative feelings over another's plight
		6. Misperceived	Gratitude that is misunderstood because of personal emotional issues
		7. Misplaced	Gratitude that is erroneously attributed to luck

THREE TYPES OF HARMFUL GRATITUDE

	MORAL QUALITY	TYPES	DEFINITION
HARMFUL GRATITUDE	Harmful gratitude lacks a moral sense because it is assocated in some way with harmful intent. Goodness is either ignored or distorted.	1. Hurtful	Gratitude expressed by the gift-recipient in order to avoid public expression of negative feelings created as a result of the gift-giver's hurtful motives.
		2. Deviant	Gratitude expressed or felt by individuals toward those who help them obtain their goals of harming others or society.
		3. Malignant	Gratitude expressed or felt by those who lead, assist, or contribute to the abuse of political power. The behaviors carried out have consequences ranging from hurtful to horrific.

we might feel the need to protect ourselves, such expressions are tarnished by their self-serving motivation.

4. Defensive gratitude is employed when we wish to conceal negative feelings. If we are running late for an important appointment, we might smile and say thank-you to a colleague to forestall an even longer discussion. If we know our conversation might lead to a heated argument, we might veer the conversation another way by saying, "Thanks for doing that," or "It means a lot to me." Defensive gratitude is sometimes seen in mental-health settings when clients in a therapy session describe their gratitude for a family member as a way to distract themselves from more negative feelings. Sometimes, however, defensive gratitude does have moral merit. If a gift from a loved one is well intended but leads to disappointment, we might express a hasty yet reassuring thanks to avert causing our loved one hurt feelings. Or, fearing for her child's safety, a mother might employ various expressions of thanks to sooth an abusive husband's ego, thereby forestalling a violent reaction.

5. If we are walking down the street on a snowy winter day and see a man twenty feet ahead of us slipping on the ice, we might feel sad that the person fell but grateful that it was not us who first came upon the patch of ice (in effect, that it was he and not we who slipped). Such a reaction is a natural one and our gratitude is decidedly mixed. Because of its guilt-evoking quality, mixed gratitude can leave us perplexed and unsure as to how we should feel. A common example is when we are grateful that an impending hurricane veers off course at the last moment, thereby sparing our city but wreaking enormous damage on another city a hundred miles away.

6. When our neediness is great or emotional state distressed, we might misinterpret another's gesture. For example, I might be invited to some function with a group or over to someone's house because others are interested in keeping costs down by dividing up the expenses, or simply because my presence provides the extra body needed for a card game. But because of my loneliness, I have misinterpreted the offer as a kindly gesture for which I express thanks.

7. Leaving a casino with a sizable sum of money might elicit an appreciation of a "paying" slot machine or the casino where the money was won. However, the sole cause of our good fortune is, simply, luck. Of course, we could express thanks to a friend who recommended the casino or who directed us to a specific slot machine with an inviting phrase such as, "Boy, I feel this is a hot one."

HARMFUL GRATITUDE

Whereas quasi-gratitude is evidenced more by the absence of goodness, harmful gratitude signifies an assault on goodness itself. When harmful gratitude takes center stage, the gift-giving process itself is corrupted, for either the giving or receiving of the gift is a source of psychological or physical harm to other human beings. Some combination of the giver's intention, the gift itself, and the expression of gratitude are, ultimately, damaging and injurious to one or more people. There exist three types of harmful gratitude: (1) hurtful gratitude, (2) deviant gratitude, and (3) malignant gratitude.

1. Though it is true that a defining feature of gratitude is the giving and receiving of gifts, it remains equally true that gift-giving itself is fraught with a widely diverging assortment of perceptions, psychological states, and conflicting emotions. "Gifts bring pride, and also envy, hatred, greed, jealousy. People are literally the creative products of the gifts they receive. But people can also be destroyed by their gifts or by the perverse effects of the gift-giving process gone awry."[27] Thus, giving a gift to flaunt wealth (triggering envy) or to display power (creating resentment) might meet with a hasty thank-you by some or sincere thanks from others, but the corruption of the gift exchange is normally apparent. The hurtful gratitude expressed usually reflects the painful feelings, as in that of a sister who expresses thanks over her brother's expensive gift to her son, while the true motive for the gift is to point out (and embarrass) his sister because of her more limited financial means.

2. Deviant gratitude is that felt by individuals who are thankful for those who aid them in their criminal actions. The

sidekick who drives a getaway car, the insider who provides illegal stock tips, or the person who efficiently organizes the neighborhood's drug distribution are the focus for the expression of deviant gratitude.

3. Finally, malignant gratitude involves a grateful response for actions that lead to harm on a significant scale. Such corrupted gratitude is most likely voiced by those in leadership positions of institutions (e.g., governments, organizations) that have the potential for bringing about great harm to large numbers of human beings.

In many instances, harmful gratitude is both sincere and heartfelt. Nonetheless, its inescapable connection to harming others defiles the gift-giving process, thereby making it diametrically opposed to, and outside the bounds of, genuine gratitude.

It is both instructive and necessary to investigate distorted gratitude. Examining its two forms (quasi-gratitude and harmful gratitude) and the various types of each establishes the inviolable nature of gratitude itself. *Only responses rooted in goodness and its accompanying gift-giving can rightfully lay claim as authentic expressions of gratitude*, thereby assuring the moral legitimacy of the statement: "I am grateful."

One other issue remains. What does goodness really mean? This question has been around since the time of the ancient Greeks and an in-depth exploration of it is beyond the scope of our discussion here.[28] Suffice it to say that the definition of goodness varies widely among people, and our pluralistic culture will never find complete consensus on some controversial issues.[29] Nonetheless, any reasonable notion of goodness that people endorse most likely would incorporate elements of compassion, justice, and respect.[30] For Christians, of course, the notion of goodness is anchored in the person and meaning of the life, death, and resurrection of Jesus and in living as his disciples in the numerous roles that define us and the many communities to which we are attached.[31] With Jesus as the source of goodness, the Christian responds to and lives life in heartfelt thanks, and it is to this theme in our final chapter that we now turn.

Chapter Five

JESUS AS GOD'S GRATITUDE AND THE CALL TO GRACED GOODNESS

Gratitude is the feeling that I have when another individual directs some unmerited act of kindness toward me that I do not deserve. It is surprise and awe that another deems one worthy of love and respect as manifested by some, perhaps even seemingly tiny action. I suppose it is also a recognition of, and appreciation for, the Good: that life possesses some unique, intrinsic dignity that cannot merely be described by random biochemical processes—that it has purpose and beauty.

—A graduate student's response to the question:
"How would you define gratitude?"

What do people mean by the word *gratitude*? This was one question that always intrigued me in the course of my surveys. As we prepare in this final chapter to understand the true nature of gratitude, it would be helpful as a starting point to reflect on what the word means for each of us. Take a few moments to complete the following exercise.

I asked several groups of people to define what gratitude meant to them. After reading several hundred definitions, I selected twenty-seven key words or phrases. Read the following list and circle the four or five that best capture *for you* your understanding of gratitude.

- Gift
- Freely given
- Undeserved
- Reach outward
- Sensitive to surroundings
- Soothing
- Changed for the better

137

- Desire to commit
- Trust
- Going out to another
- Recognition of dependence
- Warmth
- Overwhelmingly positive
- Cry of wonder
- Can bask in
- Disposed to openness
- Ready to engage
- For my good
- Quality of the heart
- Not out of duty
- Given to me
- Feel sustained
- Mindfulness of blessings
- Surprise
- Effort outside myself
- Call forth freedom
- Joyful

After circling these responses, slowly repeat several times these five words or phrases. Afterward, combine whatever sense you have of gratitude with whatever was most helpful from the previous four chapters and write below, in your own words, what the meaning of gratitude is *for you*.

_____

_____

_____

_____

Keep your definition in mind as you continue reading this chapter.

A Distinction

In my interviews with people about gratitude, I noticed an interesting twist. Starting off the conversation, nearly everyone used the words *thankful* and *grateful* interchangeably. But as people continued speaking, a number of them distinguished between the states of being thankful and having gratitude. Picking up on this distinction, I started to ask people directly, "Do you detect any difference between being thankful and being grateful?" The overwhelming majority did distinguish between *thankful* and *grateful*. Generally speaking, those interviewed associated *thankful* with ordinary customs and manners, such as "thank-you" or an acknowledgment spoken more out of duty, such as when someone extended a courtesy or offered a favor. In addition, *thankful* was usually described as focused on a specific object. Thus, if I notice my favorite pen is missing and my search leads nowhere, and a friend just happens to stop by, volunteers to help, and discovers it under a mess of cluttered papers on my desk, I am apt to acknowledge my friend's effort with a thanks. Struggling with carrying a set of heavy boxes and having someone run to open the door likewise leads me to be thankful. Yet, in the long run, such memories prove both fleeting and forgetful.

On the other hand, when people described the state of being grateful, a distinction was obvious from their voice tones and comments. To be sure, gratitude, like thankfulness, usually has a specific object; yet, its meaning, for most people, went undeniably well beyond focusing on an individual, object, or condition. One person noted that being grateful incorporates a sense that is "more lasting, more enduring" than being thankful and went on to state that "gratitude makes me feel physically different. That is how I distinguish it from thankfulness, because it is a much deeper emotion. I feel more energized, more positive, and more hopeful. It empowers me. I almost feel as if I am glowing from the inside, and this happens regardless of whether I tell the person or not." Many described the difference as levels of the same thing. "Being grateful," in the words of one person, "takes thanksgiving to another level." Instead of *thankful*, several people used the word *deeper* to describe the grateful state or, as one individual wrote: "Gratitude is deep-felt thankfulness." More specifically, whereas thankfulness was frequently linked to an object or situation, people's descriptions of gratitude pointed to a more pervasive and lasting outlook on life. Commenting on his own life, one hi-tech professional viewed gratitude as resulting from accumulating acts of kindness he had received over the years: "I think that each instance added to a pattern of being able to appreciate the acts of other people more deeply and richly with each successive event." Additionally, several people provided a moral flavor to their definitions of *gratitude* by linking it with the word *virtue* or related it to having "integrity."

These responses suggest that there exists a qualitative distinction between being thankful and having gratitude. As many frequently stated, there was *more* to being grateful than being thankful. As a way of summary, perhaps we can say that being thankful connotes a sense of appreciation aroused by an external event that is seldom memorable or meaningful, while being grateful conveys something of deeper significance and frequently includes some level of interior *transformation*.

A depth model of gratitude also accounts for the vocabulary we use to frame the gratitude experience. As gratitude deepens, we develop a grateful attitude best defined as a perceptual shift that opens up new ways to discover and understand the world. More and more we come to view the world as gift-filled. As a result, the grateful person can be described as having an "attitude of gratitude." As gratitude deepens further, we find ourselves not only employing a grateful attitude but also being disposed to gratitude (disposition). Given its transforming power, gratitude might penetrate to a depth that is not only life-altering but life-defining; that is, gratitude is not only part of who we are, but it also *is* who we are. At such a profound level, gratitude becomes our way of life and a permanent, life-transforming perspective rooted in the heart.

The Meaning of Gratitude

In light of all that has been said thus far, gratitude is best viewed as incorporating three layers of meaning: *emotion, gift,* and *goodness.* The positive feelings we experience when grateful refer to the emotional experience of gratitude. At the same time, the emotion of gratitude is *about* something. And this "something" is the meaning we provide when understanding gratitude as gift. When feeling gifted we sense ourselves as valued—we come to know ourselves as someone who matters. And to enjoy a gift frequently means to treasure something. In the process of "treasure-holding," we note something *special* taking place, which we willingly accede to and wish to sustain. As the recipient of the gift we discover ourselves as valued. (Pause for a moment and recall a time when you felt truly grateful. As you reflect on this occasion, be aware of your sense of being gifted.) Finally, the giftedness we feel becomes the key for unlocking goodness—the foundational source for the giftedness we feel—where heartfelt gratitude finds its core. To conclude, in any authentic gratitude experience, the gift we come to treasure is our own goodness.

In sum:

Positive feelings → sense of being gifted → awareness of our own goodness

Interconnecting these three layers (emotion, gift, and goodness) accounts for the popularity of gratitude. But more important for our purposes here, from this gifted sense of goodness flows a grateful giving-back whereby we share goodness by our own acts of grateful gift-giving.

Herein lies the *dynamic* of gratitude: our experience of being gifted affirms (whether explicitly or implicitly) some sense of our goodness, to which we respond by expressing our goodness through offering gifts to others, thereby creating in the process more goodness. The exchange of gifts at holiday gatherings in loving families and friendship circles illustrates this dynamic. From the Christian perspective, the best demonstration of our goodness is the graced goodness of being God's children that we share by giving to others selflessly and lovingly. Hence, gratitude is genuinely *sacramental.* Why? Because when truly grateful, what we do (gift-giving) portrays who we are: gifted. For Christians, loving acts arising from grateful hearts signify who we most truly are: graced goodness sealed in and sustained by being God's sons and daughters and Jesus' brothers and sisters. Thus, gratitude involves an ongoing, self-renewing dynamic of gift and goodness. In effect, we might say that *gratitude is the giving away of goodness.*

The interconnection between gift and goodness finds expression in the worldview of St. Ignatius Loyola. Ignatius was convinced that God gifts us through everything imaginable and thus calls us, in turn, to share selflessly the many gifts showered upon us. The central Ignatian theme of finding God in all things is premised on the nearly limitless possibilities for gratitude in everyday life (even the painful things as seen in our redemptive capacity). We can react with awe to the haunting melodies of Mozart's Piano Concerto No. 20 in D Minor, or be transfixed by the soothing gurgle of a flowing stream. Likewise, we can struggle with the intricacies of quantum mechanics, or watch intently as a spider methodically weaves its web. We might be humbled by the love another person offers us, or find serenity in the simplest or most ordinary occasion. Upon reflection and the passage of time, we may discover that a profound disappointment or deeply felt loss transforms into an avenue for growth and fresh insight. Ignatius reminds us that all these things are channels through which grace flows. Indeed, if we make time for contemplation, our focus can sharpen and we can grow to become seekers of gratitude. Contemplation helps us shed the take-it-for-granted attitude that renders us blind to God's gifting. As we increasingly absorb a grateful sense, we will be led to ask, "Why me?"—not as an expression of curiosity, but as an utterance of gratefully embraced humility. Ultimately, our focus shifts from the gift to the giver. We will recognize God's presence manifesting itself not only through the world's endless gifts but also within our very selves as the graced goodness we are—the very presence of God that we have become (1 Cor 3:16) and are now called to share.

When we experience gratitude in its deeper sense, the connection between gift and goodness lends itself to the *paradox of gratitude*: the people whom we gift (serve) do more for us than we can ever do for them. Thus, the gift-giver becomes the gift-receiver and thereby sheds the mantle of power and embraces vulnerability. For example, parents may lovingly care for a child, at times in heroically self-sacrificing ways, but they also sense that what they receive from the child is somehow far more than anything they might provide. When true friends help us in time of need, they sense their actions as gift-receiving rather than gift-giving. Good teachers know that what they teach their students is far less significant than what they learn from them. With gratitude, it seems that selfless love brings its own reward and in this way maintains energy for recurring acts of selflessness. Speaking personally, as I reflect on my twenty-five years of priesthood, the truth of this paradox seized me: even if I could not recognize it at the time, upon reflection I now understand that the students I have taught, the clients I have counseled, and the people I have ministered to over these years have done more for me than I have ever done for them.

Perhaps the most fitting testament to the paradox of gratitude is Mother Teresa. She was unconditionally a gift-giver. But this fact pales in comparison with a more dominant theme pervasive throughout her adult life. Above all, she was acutely aware that the poor to whom she devoted her life provided her gifts far more abundant than she could ever offer in return. It was this standard of humility that served to both elicit and nourish the gratitude she felt. Speaking to her sisters she noted: "Do not underestimate our practical means, the work for the poor, no matter how small and humble; they make our life something beautiful for God....[The poor] are God's most precious gift to our Society."[1] The giver became the gifted; she was the true beneficiary.

Of course, the paradox of gratitude does not mean, for example, that we yield our authority as a parent or teacher; what it does mean is that the quality of our relationships is altered profoundly. Although the parent or teacher indeed does exercise more power or possess more resources than the beneficiary of his or her kindness, in the dynamic of gift-giving, gratitude upends their mastery and brings with it a stance of vulnerability, exposing the giver to the truth that the practice of giving gifts is a humble one.

On the other hand, when our most important life commitments lack heartfelt gratitude, we lose the effects of this paradox and thus relate to others not as gifts-given-us but as burdens to bear, challenges to control, or targets for displacing our anger. In such instances, other people all too frequently become objects we use, often for our own aggrandizement. Perhaps nowhere is the absence of gratitude and its paradoxical effect more acutely and poignantly evident than in the case of child abuse. When a meaningful gift is given to us, we treasure and cherish it, yet an abusive parent is unable to perceive his or her child as gift. Similarly, the lurid stories of teachers who seduce their students are a far cry from the grateful teachers who view their students as gifts they have been given. More generally, when we violate boundaries in regards to any trusted role, our actions most likely reflect an inability to view those we are responsible for as gifts given us. Finally, the overbearing boss, the selfish colleague, the cynical spouse, the overly critical friend, the estranged family member—all are just a few instances that may indicate an absence of gratitude and of its paradoxical effect.

Using the Gratitude Paradox in Everyday Life

Make a list of the roles in your life—for example, spouse, parent, friend, child, work colleague. Now take each role and relate it to the "gratitude paradox" theme expressed in the words: "The people I relate to in this role do more for me than I could ever do for them." Thus, a woman in the roles listed above might ask:

As a wife: How is my husband ___[name]___ a gift to me? To what degree do I feel that he does more for me than I could ever do for him?

As a parent: How is my child ___[name]___ a gift to me? To what degree do I feel that he or she does more for me than I could ever do for him or her?

As a friend: How is my friend ___[name]___ a gift to me? To what degree do I feel that he or she does more for me than I could ever do for him or her?

Continue in this format until you have gone through all the roles you have listed.

Take the time to *feel the gratitude* you have for the gift you have been given in each of the roles you have listed. Ask yourself, How does experiencing each of these people as a gift-given-me influence my attitude toward them? My behavior toward them?

The significance of gratitude should be obvious by now. Yet, as Christians we must go a step further and ask how gratitude relates to Jesus. Through his life and death, Jesus represents not only the litmus test for what it means to be truly human, but also the measure for discerning everything significant and noble. "The given factor is, after all: definitive salvation-coming-from-God in Jesus of Nazareth, the crucified-and-risen One. 'It is God who delivers us in Jesus Christ' (see 2 Cor. 5:19). God saved, but in and through the man Jesus, his message, life, and death."[2] Thus, we are led to ask the question: What role might gratitude have played in Jesus' own life? As we have seen, the paradox of gratitude turns upside down conventional wisdom and social expectation with regard to power. Could this paradox in some way relate to Jesus' profound commitment as God's Son and the folly and wisdom of the cross he bore? This connection with the cross might be developed further. The Contemplation to Attain Love near the end of the *Spiritual Exercises* follows contemplations on the Lord's resurrection and death. And the links it makes between love and gratitude provoke a question: If Jesus' death was an act of love, was he grateful to die? Grateful to take up the cross we gave him? It is to these questions that we now turn.

Jesus as Gratitude

Every Lent and Easter, Christians around the world enter more intentionally and spiritually into the drama—at once dreadful and exultant—of the paschal mystery of the suffering, death, and rising of Jesus.[3] For believers, the Lenten-Easter experiences elicit sorrow and horror, contrition and reparation, joy and liberation, and gratitude. Naturally, Jesus' willingness to submit to an agonizing death by crucifixion, as well as his death-defeating victory of resurrection, evokes in us profound gratitude. But cloaked within our gratitude is a provocatively unexamined question: *Was Jesus himself grateful to die?* We are comfortable with an "obedient Jesus" who accepts and carries out his mission, a "suffering Jesus" who embraces the cross, and a "loving Jesus" who cares for us. Into every Christian's mind is instilled the picture of an obedient, suffering, and loving Jesus who, as his Father's Son, did his will. But have we ever considered the significance of what a "grateful Jesus" does for our spiritual lives? Answering this question of Jesus' gratitude has tremendous import for our lives as his disciples. While Jesus' ignoble death evokes deep gratitude from every Christian, the invitation to contemplate and *make sense* of a loving Jesus who not only suffers and dies but who is *grateful* to do so unleashes unimaginable amazement.

A Meditation on the Grateful Jesus

Take a few moments and create for yourself a quiet location that allows you the opportunity to spend time with Jesus. When you feel relaxed and comfortable, call to mind the Jesus you love. Spend a few moments with him and feel whatever feelings you have for him. As you contemplate the person of Jesus, call to mind what Jesus did for you. More specifically:

- Reflect on how much Jesus loves you.
- After a few moments, consider now how Jesus who is God suffered and gave his life for you. Focus particularly on God's suffering and death. As you ponder the immensity of this truth, pay particular attention to what you are feeling and thinking. What kind of response do you find yourself making to Jesus as you realize the depths of his love? How would you describe the gratitude you feel?
- Now consider the following: Jesus who is God suffered and died for me. But he not only suffered and died for me; he was in fact *grateful* to die for me! Be with Jesus' gratitude. What is it like knowing that God not only died for me but was also grateful to have the opportunity to offer his life for *me*? What does this grateful Jesus do for my relationship with him? What does a grateful Jesus say to me about life? About love? About suffering?
- How does knowing a grateful Jesus influence my own life as his disciple?

Of course, what we can "know" of Jesus' actual life is limited. He was an observant Jew who spent most of his life in Galilee. He most likely learned a skill from which he earned his livelihood, but at some point in his adult years he gathered around him a group of followers and preached a religious message that ultimately brought him a violent and terrible death.[4] But venturing beyond such general facts proves problematic. Despite a century-long quest to discover the historical Jesus, finding a Jesus unencumbered by faith-filled reflection is not possible. The narratives we have of Jesus are contained in the four Gospels, each of which was written by followers of Jesus from the vantage point of the life-changing resurrection experience and their belief in "Jesus as Lord." As such, the Gospels are not accounts of historical facts but narratives in which each of the writers describes from his own distinctive faith-informed perspective Jesus' life, death, and resurrection. As a consequence, we are unable to explain the mind of Jesus or investigate with any certainty his psychological life. Nonetheless, the meaning and dynamic nature of gratitude as a human experience and its close linkage to love make it one that could not help but touch Jesus who, though God, was also human.

As an observant Jew, Jesus grew up in a culture that esteemed gratitude.[5] An enduring theme of the Hebrew Bible is the gratitude owed to the Lord. Observing Jewish rituals and customs, Jesus prayed prayers filled with gratitude for the Lord's never-failing care and his forgiveness of Israel's all-too-frequent errant ways. The Book of Psalms contains a wealth of thanksgiving psalms, some communal, some personal. They include Psalm 34, with the beloved phrase "Taste and see that the Lord is good"; Psalm 138, frequently used as the Responsorial Psalm in our Thanksgiving Day liturgy; and Psalm 118, which calls on us to "give thanks to the Lord for he is good, for his love endures forever." Jesus would have prayed the thanksgiving psalms that were frequently incorporated into prayer rituals such as the Passover Seder. These hymns bear a distinctive structure. Each song recollects a painful time in Israel's past, the cry of one in need of deliverance, followed by the retelling of the Lord's saving action. The hymn concludes by offering praise for the deliverance that God's intervention brings. Indeed, in these psalms, praise to or of God is virtually synonymous with thanksgiving. As the years passed, Jesus grew thoroughly familiar with these psalms as well as the rest of the Hebrew Scriptures, which valued obedience to God as a sure sign of one's love and gratitude. Deuteronomy 30:16, for example, declares that obeying the commandments is a way of loving the Lord.

Scripture announces that the heart of Jesus' mission was proclaiming that the reign of God is at hand (Luke 19:10). The Gospel writers understandably focus on the saving message of Jesus and thus, by not giving priority to many of Jesus' personal qualities, they leave us wondering about his personal temperament and the traits he displayed in daily life. Naturally, we know Jesus as a selfless, loving human being. But what else can we say? A revealing example is laughter. Did Jesus have a sense of humor?[6] Certainly the Gospels are silent on this point. Indeed, the Gospels portray a rather serious Jesus. Yet it is hard to understand how a storyteller like Jesus, who used the hyperbole and irony of parables and riddles so effectively, and in the process fascinated, intrigued, and provoked others with his comments and insights, did not have a sense of humor. Further, the Gospel's actual humor might entirely elude us who are far removed from the first century. The spiritual author James Martin notes Daniel Harrington's comment that "the Gospels have a lot of stories about controversy and honor-shame situations. I suspect that the early readers found these stories hilarious, whereas we, in a very different social setting, miss the point entirely."[7] Moreover, Jesus' many warm friendships strongly suggest a Jesus who could not only weep at a friend's death (John 11:35), but could banter and tease as well. Just as Jesus most likely displayed a playful, lighthearted side (not to mention the fact that intuitively speaking gratitude and humor go hand in hand), the evidence is even more compelling that he was also a man of deep gratitude.

As noted above, reared in a Jewish culture that cultivated and prized gratitude and strongly encouraged a grateful outlook, he most likely approached life gratefully. His sensitivity to children and nature reveals a deep capacity to treasure innocence and simple beauty, certainly revealing his grateful sense. He enjoyed the company of others, finding companionship with his disciples and treasuring friendships, notably with Mary, Martha, and Lazarus. His friendship with (and gratitude to) Mary Magdalene is highlighted by appearing to her first after his resurrection (Mark 16:9; John 20:14).

More important, the gratitude Jesus felt finds profound expression through the Eucharist he left us. For Christians, the Eucharist represents a memorial of Jesus' approaching death. In addition, rooted in the Jewish meal-ritual of breaking bread and giving thanks, the meal itself is transformed into a "sacrifice of praise" as an expression of thanksgiving. Celebrating the Passover meal with his disciples, Jesus recounted God's saving action in bringing his people out of Egypt. The Passover meal is, in reality, a "grateful" meal, a meal of thanksgiving. However, on that fateful night, the bread and wine were no longer just symbols but became his body and blood and were offered to the Father in gratitude for the mission he was soon to bring to completion. Equally important, this ritual meal is now to happen again and again to demonstrate not only a "remembrance" of that Passover night but also a sign of Jesus' continuing role in salvation history through the worshiping community. When we participate in the Eucharist, the thanks of Jesus become our thanksgiving, too. Our gratitude is realized in the redemption he gives us through every Eucharist. His thanks of the Eucharist shows us that he holds nothing back, for his very life is our food to eat. The Jesus of the eucharistic encounter is living proof that Jesus' love for us "will pay any price, bear any burden, forgive any wrong,"[8] thereby calling us to respond gratefully through our own loving service in return. Given Jesus' overall ministry, *eucharisteō* here suggests his gratitude toward and praise of his Father for the mission with which the Father gifts him. Jesus obediently executed his mission by fulfilling the first covenant and by originating a new one that obtains for every man and woman salvation and forgiveness through our participation in God's kingdom, which Jesus now shares (Matt 26:28–29; Mark 14:25).

In their passion accounts, both Matthew and Mark relate that at his moment of death Jesus utters Psalm 22's, plaintive opening cry: "My God, my God, why have You forsaken Me?" (Matt 27:46; Mark 15:34). Yet, this psalm, which begins with a harrowing cry, turns (vv. 19–31) into a profound expression of trust and deliverance, thanksgiving and praise. Jesus' passion and death are inextricably connected with his victory over death; Jesus, like the psalmist, has been vindicated.

Gratitude and the Cross

Jesus could well feel gratitude for his Father's gifting him with his mission, despite the grisly way in which it inexorably unfolded. Was Jesus able to evoke within it the true depths of gratitude conveyed through "gift" and "goodness"? The passion accounts in the Synoptic Gospels (Matthew, Mark, and Luke) portray a tormented

Jesus, abandoned by his friends and, seemingly, by his Father as well, and yet acceding to God's will that he undergo this suffering. Who could imagine that Jesus was without fear? Yet, Jesus freely chose to go forward and embrace his anguish. What *interior experience* does Jesus undergo that allows him to face and freely accept his fate? To answer this question, let us begin by asking another: What is Jesus' gift? In what does his giftedness lie? It is his knowing and being loved by God his Father. This intimacy reflects giftedness that points to Jesus' own sense of goodness. Not even future torment could alter or eclipse Jesus' knowledge of his goodness. This goodness empowers Jesus, out of gratitude, to offer himself as gift. His understandable fear does battle with his growing gratefulness for who he is as the one who knows, as Pope Benedict has noted, "the face of God."[9] The agony in the garden reflects the *confusion* within these conflicting tensions as they play out in Jesus: fear and gift—anguish and gratitude. The affliction he endures from the torment he feels competes with the growing sense of gratitude he experiences as the one who accomplishes the most loving of all acts. Nourished by his own grateful awareness of his special relationship with God, Jesus is able to bear the benumbing fear he has felt and thereby move with all the more clarity and integrity toward the ultimate act of love that is his death, confident that he is giving away the gift that he has become. Unreservedly, he is giving away the gift that he is.

The goodness Jesus experiences through a uniquely gifted intimacy with God sustains him while holding the key to his future. To the extent that human language can describe God's action in salvation history, the dynamic of gratitude—gift given-received, goodness affirmed, and then goodness given back through gift-giving—is particularly apt. Perhaps this dynamic—summarized succinctly as the "giving away of goodness"—offers the best opportunity for us to understand the core of the paschal mystery.

Though we may be tempted to ask whether Jesus' gratitude could have led him to be grateful for the actual cross he accepted, the fact is that no one knows. Yet the profound depth of his love makes it a possibility. Of course, we must be very careful to avoid suggesting any form of spiritual masochism or finding through Jesus' gratitude-in-suffering a pretext or justification for practicing compulsive caregiving.[10] There is a big difference between masochism, or being a doormat, and willingness to suffer for those we love out of real and heartfelt love. Many years ago my mom was facing serious oral surgery. The surgeon, sensing my mom's distress, told my dad he could hold my mom's head while he performed the procedure. Dad eagerly accepted this offer. After her recovery my mom shared with me that while Dad was driving her home, he told her that he wished there was some way he could have taken her place and that he would have been glad to do this. I have never forgotten this conversation because it truly reflected the love they shared.

A number of years ago, as I was going through a personal crisis, I took a walk with a close friend to whom I recounted my dilemma. My friend turned me toward him and with his hand on my shoulder looked me in the eye and said, "Charlie, I would gladly go through anything if it would take this hurt away from you." What these examples point to is the defining feature of authentic love: we are willing to suffer for those we love and we have some grateful sense for the opportunity. Most tellingly, truly loving someone requires an attitude of willing sacrifice, one that goes beyond being merely dutiful. In other words, when love is truly present, there frequently exists a positive wish to sacrifice and feel gratitude for such an opportunity. For people we love deeply, we sometimes even "look for" such opportunities, not because we feel the need to prove something to the person we love, but simply because such sacrifices are the most authentic expression of what lies within our hearts. Such impulses to sacrifice also highlight the radical truth of St. Ignatius' lesson that love is best expressed in deeds rather than words.

So many people I interviewed in preparation for writing this book mentioned their willingness to suffer for those they loved and how such sacrifice served as a source for gratitude. This inclination points to an important insight: the *cost of gratitude*. Heartfelt gratitude, at some point, costs us. Its ultimate price is suffering.[11] No doubt while we are experiencing gratitude we describe it in positive terms. But for Christians, the truth is that at times our gratitude will inevitably find its fullest expression *only* through the suffering we endure. Filled with gratitude we care for elderly parents, sacrifice time to listen to a depressed friend, or share slender resources with those less fortunate—all people who gift us and whom we gift in return. Yet, our gratitude may cost us dearly and may involve enormous stress, great personal and physical sacrifice, or, as in Jesus' case, our very lives.

In the *Spiritual Exercises* we are led in prayerful meditation and contemplation to experience the life, death, and resurrection of Jesus and respond gratefully for his saving action and graces received. Without denying the significance of such gratitude and the vital truth that we must indeed respond gratefully for God's working in our lives, would it not also be helpful to meditate on and contemplate Jesus' gratitude? Does it not make sense to say that our focus should be *more* on Jesus' gratitude than our own? Most certainly. The more a grateful Jesus floods our consciousness and serves as object for our affection, the more we comprehend the true depth of his love for us. Yet, at the same time, as we center on the "grateful Jesus," our own gratitude swells. Perhaps herein lies the key to Lent and every other day of our Christian lives. Our goal is to "become" Jesus. As grace accomplishes this aim, our gratitude spills over into ways of living that mirror his own. As we discover and celebrate our goodness as Jesus' sisters and brothers, we are more able to gift others with this goodness. Gift, goodness, celebration, gratitude: these lie at the heart of what it means to live the Christian life—following and becoming him.

Christian Gratitude as Our Way of Life

As we become more like Jesus and experience our graced goodness as his brothers and sisters, the gratitude that deepens within us increasingly forms and informs who we are and, at its deepest level, becomes self-defining as our way of life. As gratitude takes hold as our self-definition, this grateful sense serves as a primary catalyst for how we come to know, perceive, and act in the world. This growing identity-in-gratitude leads to distinct changes. Through our graced goodness these changes are grounded in and nurtured by God's Spirit, and at the same time God's Spirit reflects this very goodness. With this in mind, below we describe some of the qualities demonstrated by gratitude as a way of life. We then sketch some distinctive themes that make such gratitude truly Christian.

GOOD ACTS

When we are truly grateful, our goodness makes moral our gratitude and invites action. To elaborate, we find ourselves carrying out the gift-giving of goodness whereby we create by our actions more goodness. Such activity becomes a moral habit (virtue).

A moving example of the moral sense of gratitude comes from a faculty member of a Midwest medical school, who wrote about the gratitude she felt from a heartrending experience during her internship year:

> "Doctor, please come look at Baby M; he's not breathing!" The baby in question had been born ten days earlier after twenty-six weeks' gestation [normal is forty weeks], weighed 600 grams (1.5 lbs), and had had a disastrous brain hemorrhage. The doctor was struggling through her fifth day as an intern, second night on call in the neonatal ICU, exhausted at 2 a.m., and anxious. Indeed, the infant only breathed when someone gently tapped the soles of his feet: absent stimulation, absent breath. The young intern doubted her ability to successfully intubate the baby and place him on the ventilator (breathing machine), but even as she considered this, a nurse stated that she thought the baby was a DNR [Do not resuscitate] and therefore should be allowed to die without intervention. A thorough review of the baby's chart, however, failed to reveal any note or order pertaining to a DNR.
>
> Reluctantly, the doctor realized that she would have to call the attending neonatologist, whom she did not yet know, for guidance. She felt inadequate, insecure, and embarrassed as she dialed, fearing a negative response. It was by now 3 a.m. and she felt incompetent. The neonatologist's sleepy voice startled her and she apologetically outlined the situation. Dr. L listened and then said quietly, "This baby has been so very sick since birth. We've had so many talks with his mother and about the seriousness of his condition and I think she knows he will probably die. We have done all that we can for this child. So,

I recommend that you just stop stimulating." The intern gasped and without thinking blurted, "Then he'll die."

Dr. L apparently heard the desperation in her voice and immediately replied, "Just keep doing what you are doing and I will be there in thirty minutes." He was. He found his intern keeping vigilance at the tiny crib. Dr. L stood closely beside her and smiled with so much gentleness and understanding that the young doctor was overwhelmed with relief and gratitude. Together they told the nurse to stop tapping the tiny feet, and waited. To everyone's amazement Baby M chose that moment to start breathing again; he lived six days longer and died peacefully.

The young doctor eventually became a faculty member herself. Always she kept the memory of that night, of the generosity, support, and kindness her mentor had shown, and she has tried to emulate his example in her own life.

I don't think anyone could deny the good lived out by the two physicians in this story. Truly, it is a story of goodness given away (the resident to the intern, the intern to Baby M). At the same time, it ratifies the paradox of gratitude, for Baby M did more for this intern than she could ever have done for him. Furthermore, the intern's gratitude continues to create goodness via the intern-turned-faculty-member's ability to harbor the memory of her mentoring attendant as she shares her gifts as a faculty member with the students she currently instructs. Truly, she now lives (role models) the gratitude she experienced that fateful night.

I did not ask the physician how religious values or a faith perspective influenced her gratitude and the ensuing good acts that followed. But what information would such a query have elicited? First of all, Baby M reminds us that in our gratitude we acknowledge God's tender care for creation, such as the lilies (Luke 12:27) or the "birds of the air" (Matt 6:26). Our actions require a watchful sensitivity that welcomes children while we learn from them their unassuming humility (Matt 19:13–15). Christian gratitude teaches us that the good we do makes a special effort to serve the powerless, the vulnerable, and the weak (which Baby M most certainly represents). Further, our gratitude makes us receptive, even eager, to embrace

Jesus' life and saving message as the guide for the good we do. With Jesus as our model, the gifts we possess are never ends in themselves; rather, we, like Jesus, use them in selfless service to build God's kingdom. Finally, our actions, sustained by the gratitude we feel, lead us confidently to explore imaginative ways to gift the world anew.

INTENTION

As a way of life, the gift-giving generated by gratitude grows more and more deliberate. Having been gifted, we desire to act with both resolve and purpose. It leads us to plan, to set goals, to be conscious of desires, and to engage life in such a way that we more effectively bring goodness to the world. Christian gratitude focuses on mission. Ever grateful to his Father and united with him, Jesus completes the mission he has been given. He is united with his Father just as he is united with us (John 14:20). Like the disciples who are sent on mission (Mark 3:14), we, too, are sent through our baptism. Filled with God's Spirit (John 14:25), our grateful sense fuels our desire to discover the mission we are given. Like John Henry Newman we can say, "God has created me to do Him some definite service; He has committed some work to me which He has not committed to another."[12]

PERCEPTION

Our gratitude also brings with it an expanding perception of gift-in-life. Slowly, yet assuredly, acquiring the self-identity of goodness (God's life in us) is intricately tied to a perceptual shift that comes to view gifts and goodness everywhere. Thus, true gratitude provides us with its own lens through which to view the world. As a consequence, the attitude we come to acquire increasingly views gifts and goodness everywhere.

In some ways, Jesus' life was about altering perceptions. He was a master at finding the paradox that shifts understanding and invites insight. Jesus tells us that if we wish to save our lives we must first lose them (Matt 16:25), that the person who wants to be first "must be last of all and servant of all" (Mark 9:35), and that we must "love our enemies" (Matt 5:44). Jesus challenges us to see in a new way and reorder our priorities. Paul refers to this as putting on the mind of Christ (Phil

2:5) so we can dedicate our lives in service. When we are grateful, we engage the world in a discerning manner, inquiring where the Spirit is leading us and seeking new insight into our experiences so that we might grow and mature in Christ-likeness (Eph 4:15–16).

MEMORY

A grateful memory is crucial to any deepening of gratitude. Even a difficult life history, full of incidents that derail so many opportunities for gratitude, rarely completely subverts a grateful memory of gratitude (recall Ashley in the last chapter). Memories of adversity are acknowledged for what they are, but they fail to control us. As our gratitude increases, positive memories become a reservoir from which we can draw upon when facing misfortune and pain. We are confident that the gift that defines us can be given away, even though the past might be troubling, the present not always understood, and the future unknown.

A grateful memory helps to explain the inner peace and contentment that is possible with advancing age. When many older persons say that they have "no real regrets" about their lives, they are expressing gratitude for the many opportunities the have had to give their goodness away. In this sense, then, *gratitude, more than any other, is the defining emotion of adulthood.*

Jesus' life was the living of grateful memory. From its earliest days, the church's most pressing task was to discover how to keep alive the memory of Jesus that was enshrined in the eucharistic encounter ("Do this in remembrance of me"; 1 Cor 11:24). Our Christian gratitude motivates us to examine seriously how what we say and do, both communally and individually, preserves his memory. "If we really believe that whoever has seen and heard Jesus has seen and heard the Father, then keeping alive Jesus' memory is the noblest and most important task that any of us can take up and carry out."[13]

OPENNESS

Gratitude fosters in us a growing openness. If we view the world as good and as gift and recognize our call to be gift-givers, if our memories are reassuring and point the way to hope-filled lives, if our life goal is to experience and to share our gifts, then we naturally engage life with openness and zeal. If I acknowledge that goodness exists (both in the world and in *me*), and I possess the power to give it away, then I am radically open to life and its possibilities. We don't always know where our efforts might lead us, but gratitude encourages us to active engagement in the world, wherever the path might lead. Thus, gratitude makes a life of Christian discipleship all the more viable, for we are truly God's messengers and we incarnate his presence wherever we are. Our openness to the world imitates that of Jesus, who often sought out the outcasts (e.g., tax collectors, sinners, lepers). Further, he himself was sometimes genuinely surprised by the responses he encountered from people such as the centurion (Matt 8:5–13) or the Canaanite woman (Matt 15:21–28). In Christian gratitude we remain open to the possibility of surprise and the "new" ways in which God might be speaking.

From a communal perspective, the church also strives for such openness. Always remaining faithful to (and grateful for) Jesus' message and the mission he has given us, the community of faith must continually seek how that message might be better understood and communicated.

SUFFERING

A truly grateful heart rejects unconditionally any notion of suffering for its own sake. But deeply felt gratitude will most certainly not cower in the face of suffering. Gratitude means that we can perceive our suffering as having been transformed into a gift; we see the redemptive power of suffering through redemption.[14]

For Jesus, this is of course realized through the incarnation where "the Word became flesh" (John 1:14). Jesus, fully human, "emptied himself" (Phil 2:7), experiencing in the process the temptations, disappointments, and afflictions that go with being human. We confront personal failure, anguish over rejections, reel from loss, or struggle to resist the painful lies of an aggrieved childhood: these are only a few examples when our lives make little sense. But a gratitude that is heartfelt will resist such sufferings from ultimately triumphing or defining us indefinitely. The cost of gratitude means at some point in time we truly can see that our suffering itself has been transforming, becoming itself a gift. We know the resurrection ushers in a deeper joy, implanting a hope-filled perspective.

The following diagrams provide an overview and summarize how various qualities associated with gratitude come to deepen and find greatest fruition as a way of life. As the various qualities deepen within us, our gratitude finds new depth.

Taking these qualities and living out our graced goodness as Jesus' brothers and sisters transforms our gratitude into a decidedly "Christian" gratefulness. Christian gratitude turns our grateful living into a truly Christian way of life. Christian gratitude might best be defined as *gratefully experiencing the grace-filled presence of Jesus within us, which leads us to engage our world humbly and openly while discovering, in the process, that the grace-filled goodness we are is the very goodness we seek to give away.* In its fullest expression, Christian gratitude is *the* Christian way of life.

Gratitude's Internal Gaze

We conclude our discussion of gratitude with a final question: Why is gratitude so universally attractive? A partial answer lies in the many themes discussed in this book, such as the positive feelings it triggers. But another important explanation lies in gratitude's self-centering moment or what I term its internal gaze.

An exceptionally fitting portrayal of this truth was captured by one writer when he was chaperoned around England at the age of thirteen in the company of his two sisters. Stopping at a souvenir shop in Stratford-upon-Avon, he purchased a few small items.

> The elderly lady behind the counter took my money, returned me some change, and then withdrew from the display case a tiny one-square-inch edition of *Romeo and Juliet* and, smiling, gave it to me. A gift. I took the six-pence she had just given me in change, and deposited it in her hand: a reciprocal gift. Once outside, I received a resonant rebuke from my teacher. I had done an offensive thing, she informed me. A gift is a gift, she said. I must learn to accept gifts. They are profaned by any attempt at automatic reciprocity.[15]

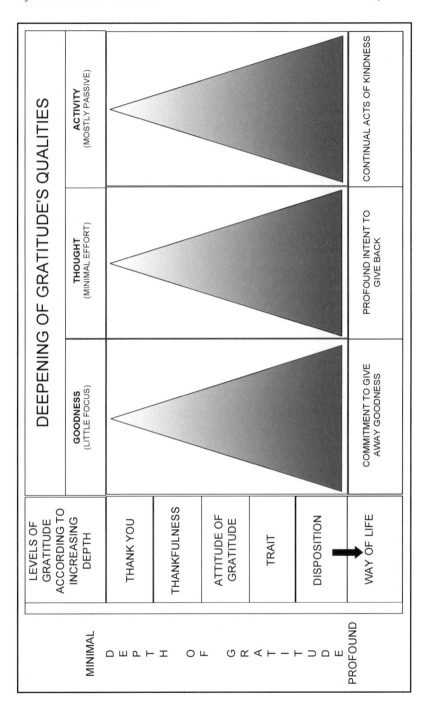

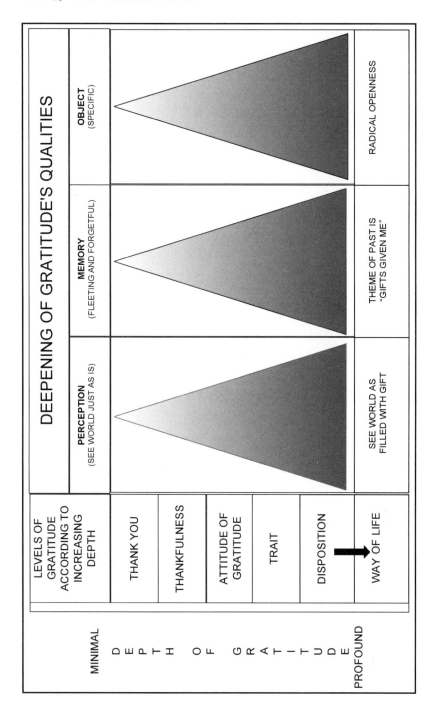

DEEPENING OF GRATITUDE'S QUALITIES

LEVELS OF GRATITUDE ACCORDING TO INCREASING DEPTH	PERCEPTION (SEE WORLD JUST AS IS)	MEMORY (FLEETING AND FORGETFUL)	OBJECT (SPECIFIC)
THANK YOU			
THANKFULNESS			
ATTITUDE OF GRATITUDE			
TRAIT			
DISPOSITION			
WAY OF LIFE	SEE WORLD AS FILLED WITH GIFT	THEME OF PAST IS "GIFTS GIVEN ME"	RADICAL OPENNESS

MINIMAL

DEPTH OF GRATITUDE

PROFOUND

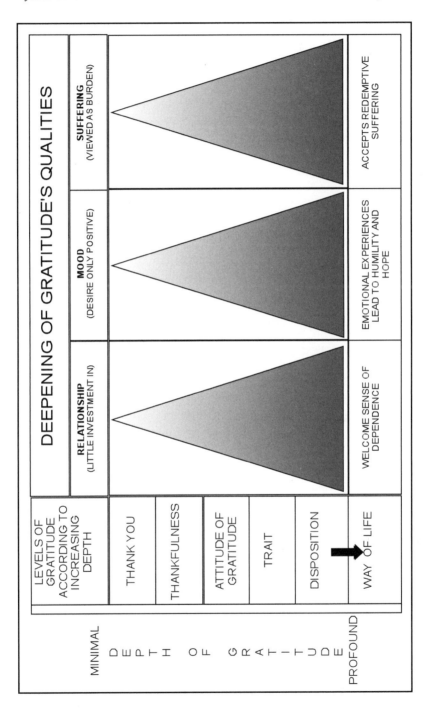

There is a valuable nugget of wisdom in the writer's recounting of this early adolescent experience. He was given a gift. It was not something that required repayment. In a true sense, there was nothing to do but *be* with the gift in all its delight. At that moment, anything else demanding of him some obligation to reciprocate appeared woefully inadequate, even intrusively so.

This very ordinary event teaches us that an integral, fundamental feature of the gratitude experience is that centering moment where the gift itself is simply relished for what it is. Such moments might be fleeting or last years. Any experience of heartfelt gratitude triggers this internal gaze, this cherished moment. Thus, strolling and feeling alive, absorbing oneself in a favorite painting, recalling someone's kindness, marveling at a child's self-discovery, relishing the security of long-standing friendship, attending to prayer, connecting with a moment in one's life that produced insight, basking in joy after hearing the words "I love you"—all are sources for gratitude and this interior moment we savor. One friend remarked to me about the gratitude he felt while working at a soup kitchen. His eyes caught a glimpse of a mother's face as she accepted the food offered her but whose attention was focused not on the food but on the child she carried tenderly in her arms. His gratitude seemed most to come alive by simply relishing the moment he had for witnessing the love of a mother for her child. It is this cherished sense of just being with the gift we have been given—an almost turning inward (hence the "internal gaze")—that makes the shift from gift-recipient to ourselves as gift-givers both effortless and desirable.

The internal gaze of gratitude invites, exposes, and summons us to face squarely the goodness that lies within us. In this sense, gratitude is, essentially, the sustaining affirmation of our goodness. We perceive the generosity of others' gifting us as good, which thereby sparks in us the core reality that goodness lies within. The gift confirms what we are already—our goodness—a truth most of us spend a lifetime forgetting. An eighty-year-old retired teacher said it best: "Isn't it true that we all too often feel it is up to us to make sure that goodness exists? We naturally and mistakenly think we are that goodness by all our endeavors, that we are responsible for getting the goodness to come about by what we do." Gratitude reminds us, then, of the continually forgotten fact that our goodness consists not in what we do but in *who we are*. It is from this sense of inner goodness that we are freely able to give back and thus give away our goodness, the hallmark of gratitude.

Sadly, we frequently seek this goodness elsewhere. We advertise our goodness by our actions and mistakenly equate goodness with results. For some it is always trying to be the best, which too often becomes a life of all-consuming competition. Others construct a false goodness through the compulsion to do good things and end up being compulsive caregivers. What gratitude effectively does is shred the distorted myth that goodness is to be found from attaining, doing, and achieving.

A life of *Christian* gratitude transforms this internal gaze from a cherished moment of delight to the conscious joy of knowing we are loved by God, who loved us first (1 John 4:10), totally and unconditionally. We are loved just for who we are, with no strings attached. If we are truly to become Jesus' disciples, we must take seriously the internal gaze of Christian gratitude. Far too frequently, having absorbed our culture's frantic pace and its never-ending message to achieve, we hurriedly acknowledge God's love while already planning another good work to take on. As a result, we short-circuit the transforming nature of our graced goodness. "We deny God's transforming influence if we rush to return love to God or to spread love to our neighbor. Sitting with eyes closed and hands open, we let God's love touch and move us: there begins our salvation."[16] By fostering our internal gaze, Christian gratitude resets our priorities. It reorients us to relish and affirm above all God's love for us. Only then do we truly have the freedom to love God as we desire and cooperate with his call to live loving lives (1 John 4:21). Correspondingly, his love nurtures our goodness and in the process allows for and soothes our failures and suffering while leading us to respond in selfless service. Our gratitude serves as the centripetal force, pulling us back so that we recognize again and again that our goodness resides as *graced* goodness. Yet the temptation to seek our goodness elsewhere always remains. When our vision clouds, we succumb to focusing on some goodness we can acquire, and we set up for ourselves intolerable odds and unbearable burdens. Just think of all the things that people do to achieve some measure or sense of goodness for themselves:

We struggle to gain prestigious credentials. We read books and take courses on how to make a good impression. We discard clothes that are not worn out and buy new, more fashionable ones. We work hard to devise self-serving explanations for failure or mishaps and fight to make others take the blame. We go hungry to make ourselves fashionably thin. We rehearse conversations or presentations in advance and ruminate about them afterwards to try and imagine what went wrong. We undergo cosmetic surgery. We endlessly seek information about other people so we can have a basis for comparing ourselves. We engage in fistfights with people who impugn our respectability and superiority. We grope desperately for rationalizations. We blush and brood when someone makes us look foolish. We buy endless magazines advising us how to look better, make love better, succeed at work or play or dieting, and say clever things.[17]

One of the most stressful (and psychically depleting) aspects of twenty-first-century living is the pressure to construct and achieve some sense of personal goodness. This becomes so taxing and wearying that we spend our lives chasing unrealistic dreams and become a stranger to the deepest part of our humanity. A middle-aged professional facing personal failure said it well when he told me, "I have spent my life thus far always trying to perform and do good and thinking that this makes me good. Having failed, I now have to realize that I must first search for goodness within me. I must start with my own goodness because only then does doing good make any sense." As this person altered his thinking, he grew more comfortable with himself and came slowly to recognize the goodness that was in him through God's love and his need to be attentive to that love through cultivating his spiritual life. His growing gratitude to God, sparking his own sense of goodness by being loved unconditionally, allowed him to engage the world anew with a greater sense of freedom. Of course, we do have to engage the world, garner respect, make impressions, persuade others, look presentable, and demonstrate competence if we are to use our God-given talents to help build his kingdom. The danger lurks when these various activities become themselves our goal, the source of our sense of self-fulfillment, or the meaning for our lives. It is here that gratitude is key, for it helps us to keep any talent, desire, or course of action in its proper perspective.

Gratitude, ultimately, provides liberation and freedom. When truly felt, it frees us from the false selves and bogus misconceptions that rule our lives. A grateful heart both speaks and instructs us in a way no other human experience can. Its truth rests—as we savor the gift—in knowing our goodness. There is a spiritual maxim (often phrased incorrectly) that very much expresses the message of gratitude: Work as if everything depends upon God, and pray as if everything depends upon you.[18] The message of this spiritual truth is the following: What is important is our relationship with God. Nourish it, cultivate it, attend to it. We must first and foremost love God while letting God love us. It must always be the starting point. Moreover, scientific research conducted by psychologists indicates (not surprisingly) that attention to and cultivation of prayer makes us more grateful.[19]

The most unshakable truth a Christian can embrace is, simply, that God loves me. With this foundation, if we follow the Lord and try to do his will, then whether we accomplish much or little, whether we are praised highly or ignored, whether we fulfill our dreams or struggle with disappointments is relatively unimportant, in that none of these hold the meaning of our lives. What gives our lives their purpose is our goodness, which resides in the grace-filled presence of being God's sons and daughters, Jesus' brothers and sisters.

Fostering Graced Goodness

St. Paul describes believers as "saints." He believed that a Christian's call in life was quite simple: live a holy life. From the perspective of gratitude, holiness is, simply, our graced goodness. Every Christian is graced goodness in the flesh. Christian tradition has many wonderful phrases and images that reflect this holiness and fittingly portray our relationship with God—for example, a son or daughter of God, a sister or brother of Jesus, a person made in the image of God, an earthen vessel, a temple of the Holy Spirit, a saint, a dwelling place for God, an example of God's handiwork.

- Is there another phrase you find helpful? If so, add it to the list above.
- Take the sentence stem "I am…" and apply it to each of the phrases in the list (e.g., "I am a son of God," etc.) After repeating each of the sentences, slowly take the phrase that most appeals to you and simply sit with it. Repeat the phrase slowly several times and feel its effects on you.
- Then slowly repeat the phrase "This is my goodness" as you are identifying with the phrase you have chosen.
- When you are ready, express some words of gratitude to God for the graced goodness you are as conveyed by your chosen phrase.
- Conclude by spending a few moments reflecting on how you can give your goodness away.

THE VOCABULARY OF GRATITUDE

The eighteen phrases below express the language of gratitude. It is helpful to review them periodically and reflect on how we have recently discovered examples of each in our own lives. Such continual reflection helps keep our gratitude fresh and alive.

Art of gratitude. Each of us lives Christian discipleship in very concrete ways in such varied roles as friend, spouse, sibling, colleague, teammate, and so on. When we journey with others in any specific role, we practice the "art" of gratitude when we invite others to consider how the various experiences of their lives are opportunities to be grateful. When we invite others to gratitude, we do so prudently and always with respect in regard to their situation and interior state.

Christian gratitude. As believers we experience the grace-filled presence of Jesus within us, which leads us to engage our world humbly and openly while discovering in the process that the grace-filled goodness we are is the very goodness we seek to give away.

Consciousness of gratitude. When we are aware of our gratitude. Such awareness takes effort. We must "practice" gratitude if we are to become the grateful persons we desire to be.

Cost of gratitude. As we increasingly find ourselves grateful, we discover its "cost," which is suffering. Gratitude allows for suffering, provides it meaning, and, at times, welcomes it.

Graced goodness. Our lives as God's sons and daughters and Jesus' brothers and sisters. It is this core sense of goodness that we give away through selfless service to others. Gratitude thus takes on a sacramental perspective, for through our actions we reflect who we most truly are: God's graced presence in this world.

Grateful reasoning. Mindfully reflecting on our commitments in order to discover the depth of our gratitude.

Gratitude as a way of life. The goal of living gratefully. The more we desire and practice gratitude in daily life, the more it becomes part of who we are. As gratitude over the years deepens within us, we desire to come to the point (goal) where gratitude is not only what we do but who we are. In other words, gratitude now defines us.

Gratitude's depth. The degree to which gratitude has deepened within us. For example, we can periodically act gratefully and slowly come to the point where we view the world gratefully (an attitude of gratitude). With increasing gratitude we might come to a point where we are more and more disposed to gratitude (gratitude disposition). Our goal is to live gratitude as a way of life (see above).

Gratitude's dynamic. Gratitude in action. The ongoing process whereby the one who is gifted (gift-receiver) and who experiences goodness turns outward by sharing gifts with others, thereby giving away goodness. This is why we can say that gratitude is, in its essence, the giving away of goodness.

Gratitude's internal gaze. The inner, positive sense we feel when grateful, which at least for a moment (though it can endure for years) is self-absorbing. Eventually, this inner focus turns outward toward the one who has gifted us and the desire to share our goodness with others through our own gift-giving.

Gratitude's surplus. The felt-sense of gratitude includes a sense of something "extra." Practically speaking this sense helps buffer us and weathers well the ill effects of stressors, thereby diminishing the tendency to react negatively. When the surplus of gratitude absorbs the adversities we encounter, we find our lives cushioned in such a way that we can more achieve our goals and be the people we desire to be.

Immunity of gratitude. The protection the gratitude surplus (see above) provides as we live everyday life.

Invitation to gratitude. When we say that gratitude invites us, we mean the possibility that virtually any experience—no matter how positive or negative—can be a source for gratitude. Implicit in this notion is the need to embrace our lives and all that has happened to us and acknowledge both the good and the bad in our life histories. Also, this invitation requires we have time for reflection and solitude so we can discover our own gifts as well as the world's gifts.

Layers of gratitude. The meaning of gratitude is found in its three layers (levels)s: emotion, gift, and goodness.

Lens of appreciation. Gratitude alters our perceptions, allowing us to view the world as filled with goodness and gift.

Paradox of gratitude. When we help others—whether it be through ministering, teaching, parenting, mentoring, or simply through the commonplace relationships found in friendship—those who receive our kindness often express their gratitude. However, irony exists because as the gift-giver we feel gratitude to them. This paradox is summed up in the statement: the people we serve do more for us than we ever do for them. The value of this gratitude paradox is its ability to view others as "gift." By adopting the perspective of others gifting us, we avoid or place limits on relating to them from a position of arbitrary power or using them for our own needs. Rather, a gift is something we find precious and thus treat with care and respect.

Structure of gratitude. Gratitude contains four elements. When grateful we experience (a) a positive sense because (b) we recognize the kindly intent of another to aid us thereby leading us to (c) experience our goodness (from the gift-giving offered us) and which (d) leads us to respond in a similar fashion (our own gift-giving).

Surprise of gratitude. We can feel grateful from almost any experience, including the ordinary and the painful, at any time, even when we least expect it.

NOTES

Chapter One

1. George H. Gallup, Jr., "Thanksgiving: America's Saving Grace" (paper presented at the National Day of Prayer Breakfast, Thanks-Giving Square, Dallas, May 1998).

2. John T. Noonan, Jr., *The Lustre of Our Country* (Berkeley: University of California Press, 1998).

3. Robert Estrin, "U.S. Racism Alive and Well Study Warns," *The Denver Post*, October 2, 1999, 9A.

4. "Thanksgiving in the U.S.A.," http://www.thanksgiving. org/html/traditions/national.html (retrieved September 9, 1999). This article contains numerous factual data on Thanksgiving. See also the website http://www.Gratefulness.org.

5. Oprah Winfrey, "The Attitude of Gratitude," *O: The Oprah Magazine* (November 2000), 49.

6. Frank Reale, SJ, "Provincial's Corner," *Forty-Five Eleven* 4 (November 2000): 1.

7. Peter Jennings, "Giving Thanks as an American," *USA Weekend*, November 21–23, 2003, 9.

8. "Thanksgiving in the World," http://www.thanksgiving. org/html/traditions/world.html (retrieved October 5, 1999).

9. For a summary of the research on gratitude and happiness, see Philip C. Watkins, "Gratitude and Subjective Well-Being," in *The Psychology of Gratitude*, ed. Robert A. Emmons and Michael E. McCullough (New York: Oxford University Press, 2004), 167–92.

10. Quoted in Robert A. Emmons and Michael E. McCullough, "Counting Blessings Versus Burdens: An Experimental Investigation of Gratitude and Subjective Well-Being in Daily Life," *Journal of Personality and Social Psychology* 84 (2003): 378.

11. G. K. Chesterton, *St. Francis of Assisi* (New York: Doran, 1924), 114.

12. Solomon Schimmel, "Gratitude in Judaism," in *The Psychology of Gratitude*, ed. Robert A. Emmons and Michael E. McCullough (New York: Oxford University Press, 2004), 54.

13. Derek Bok, "Ethics, the University, and Society," *Harvard Magazine* 91 (May–June 1991): 39.

14. Positive mood states are frequently associated with caring behaviors. See Robert B. Cialdini, Douglas T. Kenrick, and Donald J. Baumann, "Effects of Mood on Prosocial Behavior in Children and Adults," in *The Development of Prosocial Behavior*, ed. Nancy Eisenberg (New York: Academic Press, 1982), 339–59.

15. Edward J. Harpham, "Gratitude in the History of Ideas," in *The Psychology of Gratitude*, ed. Robert A. Emmons and Michael E. McCullough (New York: Oxford University Press, 2004), 21.

16. National Advisory Mental Health Council, *Basic Behavioral Science Research for Mental Health* (Washington, DC: U.S. Department of Health and Human Services, 1995), 25.

17. Nico H. Frijda, "The Laws of Emotion," *American Psychologist* 43 (1988): 354.

18. For a discussion of twenty-first-century stressors, mental health, and the recent recession, see M. Price, "The Recession Is Stressing Men More Than Women," *APA Monitor* 40 (July/August 2009): 10.

19. In a major study on the relationship between religion and mental disorder, it was found that having a sense of thankfulness—a dimension of religiosity—was associated with a reduced risk of psychiatric disorder. See Kenneth S. Kendler et al., "Dimensions of Religiosity and Their Relationship to Lifetime Psychiatric and Substance Use Disorders," *American Journal of Psychiatry* 160 (2003): 496–503.

20. Daniel Costello, "Incidents of 'Desk Rage' Disrupt America's Offices," *Wall Street Journal*, January 16, 2001, B1.

21. For the benefits of gratitude, see Robert A. Emmons and Michael E. McCullough, "Counting Blessings Versus Burdens," *Journal of Personality and Social Psychology* 84 (2003): 377–89.

22. Jennifer Barrett Ozois, "At Risk," http://www.msnbc.msn.com/id/7184214/site/newsweek/ (retrieved: March 16, 2005).

23. Jane E. Brody, "Personal Health: Feel Sleepy in the Middle of the Day? You're Probably Not Getting Enough Rest at Night," *New York Times* (National Edition), January 26, 1994, B7.

24. I wish to acknowledge the scholarship of Mihaly Csikszentmihalyi, whose study of "flow," "psychic energy," and "consciousness" has influenced my own thinking. See Mihaly Csikszentmihalyi, *Flow: The Psychology of Optimal Experience* (New York: Harper & Row, 1990).

25. For a discussion of "autopilot consciousness" and its effects on daily life, see Charles M. Shelton, *Achieving Moral Health* (New York: Crossroad Publishing, 2000), 62–75.

26. Dirk Johnson, "A Generation's Anthem: 'Smells Like Teen Pressure,'" *New York Times* (National Edition), January 1, 2000, 22.

27. See David G. Myers and Ed Diener, "Who Is Happy?" *Psychological Science* 6 (1995): 10–19; and Mihaly Csikszentmihalyi, "If We Are So Rich, Why Aren't We Happy?" *American Psychologist* 54 (1999): 821–27.

28. Robert A. Emmons and Michael E. McCullough, "Highlights from the Research Project on Gratitude and Thankfulness: Dimensions and Perspectives on Gratitude," http://www.psy.miami.edu/faculty/mmccullough/Gratitude_Page.htm (retrieved March 3, 2005). See also Michael E. McCullough, Robert A. Emmons, and Jo-Ann Tsang, "The Grateful Disposition: A Conceptual and Empirical Topography," *Journal of Personality and Social Psychology* 82 (2002): 112–27.

29. John Templeton Foundation, *Kindling the Science of Gratitude: The Humble Initiative Approach, A Symposium* (Radnor, PA: John Templeton Foundation Press, 2000), 1.

30. Robert A. Emmons, *The Psychology of Ultimate Concerns* (New York: The Guilford Press, 1999), 172.

31. Trish Hall, "Seeking a Focus on Joy in the Field of Psychology," *New York Times* (National Edition), April 28, 1998, B10.

32. Martin E. P. Seligman, "President's Column: Positive Social Science," *APA Monitor* 29 (April 1998): 2.

33. Martin E. P. Seligman, "President's Column: What Is the 'Good Life'?" *APA Monitor* 29 (October 1998): 10.

34. David G. Myers and Ed Diener, "Who Is Happy?": 10.

35. As we will read later in chapter 5, gratitude is best understood and conceptualized as a depth model. In the pages ahead, when I use phrases such as "heartfelt," "true gratitude," "authentic gratitude," or "genuine gratitude," I am referring to gratitude in a deeper and more profound sense. Such depictions of gratitude reflect the essence of gratitude, which corresponds to the notions of gift-giving and goodness.

36. For an overview of gratitude from a conceptual level, see Robert A. Emmons and Charles M. Shelton, "Gratitude and the Science of Positive Psychology," in *Handbook of Positive Psychology*, ed. C. R. Snyder and S. J. Lopez (New York: Oxford University Press, 2002), 459–71; and Robin C. Roberts, "The Blessings of Gratitude: A Conceptual Analysis," in *The Psychology of Gratitude*, ed. Robert A. Emmons and Michael McCullough (New York: Oxford University Press, 2004), 58–78.

Chapter Two

1. Robert A. Emmons and Charles M. Shelton, "Gratitude and the Science of Positive Psychology," in *Handbook of Positive Psychology*, ed. C. R. Snyder and S. J. Lopez (New York: Oxford University Press, 2002), 459.

2. Ibid., 460.

3. Ibid.

4. I am indebted to John Ridgway, SJ, for this fact.

5. Robert A. Emmons, *Thanks! How the New Science of Gratitude Can Make You Happier* (New York: Houghton Mifflin, 2007), 97–99.

6. Gerald M. Fagin, SJ, "Stirred to Profound Gratitude," *Review for Religious* 54 (1995): 237–52.

7. William W. Meissner, SJ, *Ignatius of Loyola: The Biography of a Saint* (Yale University Press, 1992), 87.

8. Wilkie Au, "Ignatian Service: Gratitude and Love in Action," *Studies in the Spirituality of Jesuits* 40 (Summer 2008).

9. Ibid., 8.

10. Meissner, *Ignatius of Loyola*, 293–94.

11. Jonathan Lear, *Open Minded: Working Out the Logic of the Soul* (Cambridge, MA: Harvard University Press, 1998), 24.

12. Ignatius's stress on felt-knowledge, which brings together the experiential/affective mode of knowing with a rational/analytic knowing, finds support in contemporary psychological theorizing, which maps out knowing into two domains: the emotional and the rational. See Seymour Epstein, "Integration of the Cognitive and Psychodynamic Unconscious," *American Psychologist* 49 (1994): 709–24.

13. Of course, it is helpful here to interject that any commitment we have in relationship involves two people. As such, if one is not appreciative of the other, then any grateful reasoning regarding the relationship is to some degree thwarted, proving less than satisfying. A spouse or friend who, for whatever reasons, fails to respond lovingly will impede the promise that grateful reasoning offers. In a similar vein, any vocation or career choice that is felt as unsatisfying undermines our ability to reason gratefully to the fullest degree possible. In such instances, we must draw from grateful reasoning what we can and then find in such reasoning realistic hope and fortitude to be the most loving men and women we desire to be. Above all, grateful reasoning must not be used to avoid difficult and painful decisions that we might have to consider making after prayerful discernment and adequate consultation regarding significant life choices.

14. One comment needs to be made. When we "rank order" something, we are indicating our own preference for one idea over another. Thus, the reason to which we assign number 1 takes priority (is preferred) over the reason that we rank as 2, and so on. Thus, with this chart we are saying that the reason assigned a 1 draws the most gratitude, the reason assigned a 2 provides the second greatest degree of gratitude, and so on.

Chapter Three

1. Ten words were asked for, but because of a tie, twelve rather than ten words are listed.

2. Mihaly Csikszentmihalyi, *Flow: The Psychology of Optimal Experience* (New York: Harper & Row, 1990), 36–39.

3. For an overview of the relationship between narcissism and gratitude, see Robert A. Emmons, *Thanks! How the New Science of Gratitude Can Make You Happier* (New York: Houghton Mifflin, 2007), 148–52.

4. Lisa Farwell and Ruth Wohlwent-Lloyd, "Narcissistic Processes: Optimistic Expectation, Favorable Self-Evaluation, and Self-Enhancing Attributions," *Journal of Personality* 66 (1998): 65–83.

5. Robert N. Bellah et al., *Habits of the Heart: Individualism and Commitment in American Life* (Berkeley, CA: University of California Press, 1985).

6. This quotation is part of a summary of Sheila Dierks' views as expressed in Cate Terwilliger, "Many Thanks," *The Denver Post*, November 21, 1999, 9H.

7. Mihaly Csikszentmihalyi, "If We Are So Rich, Why Aren't We Happy?" *American Psychologist* 54 (1999): 821.

8. A delicate moral issue arises when we compare our own more-advantaged situation to the unfortunate plight of others. In a sense we are "using" others' misfortunes to make ourselves "feel good." Moreover, it is their adversity that brings about our own relief and, no doubt, joy that we escaped the calamity that befell them. In essence, to a degree we benefit by "using" others. When reflecting upon the moral unease that surfaces when making such comparisons, the following comments should prove helpful: First, from an evolutionary standpoint (optimizing one's chances of survival), such comparisons are inevitable and probably, to a degree, unavoidable. Second, there is need to balance our relief at having been spared such misfortune with empathy and concern for those who have suffered. Third, we need to be clear in our own mind that we genuinely wish that the adverse or unfortunate situation encountered by others had never occurred.

9. Richard Reeves, *President Nixon: Alone in the White House* (New York: Simon & Schuster, 2001), 13.

10. It is common counseling practice to encourage clients to write down or make lists of people, events, or things for which they are grateful.

11. This idea is explained in Cate Terwilliger, "Many Thanks," 9H.

12. Laurence Thomas, "The Reality of the Moral Self," *The Monist* 76 (1993): 10.

13. Ibid., 8–14.

14. For a discussion of various issues surrounding the extent of gratitude that children might show parents, see Stephen G. Post, "What Children Owe Parents: Ethics in an Aging Society," *Thought* 64 (1989): 315–24; and Suzanne Selig, Tom Tomlinson, and Tom Hickey, "Ethical Dimensions of Intergenerational Reciprocity: Implications for Practice," *The Gerontologist* 31 (1991): 624–30.

15. Laurence Thomas, "The Reality of the Moral Self," 9.

16. Terrance C. McConnell, *Gratitude* (Philadelphia: Temple University Press, 1993), 58.

17. Fred R. Berger, "Gratitude," in *Vice and Virtue in Everyday Life*, ed. Christina Hoff Sommers (Orlando, FL: Harcourt Brace Jovanovich, 1985), 205.

18. Paul F. Camenisch, "Gift and Gratitude in Ethics," *The Journal of Religious Ethics* 9 (Spring 1981): 10.

19. Beverley Fehr and James A. Russell, "Concept of Emotion Viewed from a Prototype Perspective," *Journal of Experimental Psychology: General* 113 (1984): 464.

20. James J. Gross, "Emotion and Emotional Regulation," in *Handbook of Personality: Theory and Research*, ed. Lawrence A. Pervin and Oliver P. John (New York: Guilford Press, 1999), 525.

21. Susan Shott, "Emotion and Social Life: A Symbolic Interactionist Analysis," *American Journal of Sociology* 84 (1979): 1317–34.

22. Paul Ekman, "An Argument for Basic Emotions," *Cognition and Emotion* 6 (1992): 175–78.

23. Shua Sommers and Corinne Kismitzki, "Emotions and Social Context: An American-German Comparison," *British Journal of Sociology* 27 (1988): 35–49.

24. Norma Haan, Eliane Aerts, and Bruce A. B. Cooper, *On Moral Grounds: The Search for Practical Morality* (New York: NYU Press, 1985), 147.

25. Risako Ide, "'Sorry for Your Kindness': Japanese Inter-actional Ritual in Public Discourse," *Journal of Pragmatics* 29 (1995): 509–29.

26. Arjun Appadurai, "Gratitude as a Social Mode in South India," *Ethos* 13 (1985): 240.

27. Clare Brant, "Communication Patterns in Indians: Verbal and Non-Verbal," *Annals of Sex Research* 6 (1993): 259–69.

28. Robert A. Emmons and Charles M. Shelton, "Gratitude and the Science of Positive Psychology," in *Handbook of Positive Psychology*, ed. C. R. Snyder and Shane J. Lopez (New York: Oxford University Press, 2002), 460.

29. Ibid., 461.

30. Charles M. Shelton, *Morality of the Heart* (New York: Crossroad, 1990).

31. Richard S. Lazarus and Bernice N. Lazarus, *Passion and Reason: Making Sense of Our Emotions* (New York: Oxford University Press, 1994), 118.

32. As before, ten words were asked for, but because of a tie, eleven words are listed here.

33. I am indebted to Professor Carroll Izard for his comments to me on "co-occurring emotions" (personal communication, March 23, 1999).

34. See, for example, Susan L. Holak and William J. Havlena, "Feelings, Fantasies, and Memories: An Examination of the Emotional Components of Nostalgia," *Journal of Business Research* 42 (1998): 217–26.

35. Hewitt B. Clark, James T. Northrop, and Charles T. Barkshire, "The Effects of Contingent Thank-You Notes on Case Managers' Visiting Residential Clients," *Education and Treatment of Children* 11 (1988): 45–51; and Bruce Rind and Prashant Brodia, "Effects of Server's 'Thank You' and Personalization on Restaurant Tipping," *Journal of Applied Social Psychology* 25 (1995): 745–51.

36. Dan P. McAdams, *The Person: An Introduction to Personality Psychology* (Orlando, FL: Harcourt Brace & Co., 1994), 755–56.

37. After escaping harm, people often engage in imagined thinking that demonstrates recognition that "it could have happened to me." Such thinking, termed *counterfactual thought*, focuses on what could have been otherwise. Its presence in human thinking arises so commonly that it must be considered an important avenue for the development of gratitude. See Karl Halvor Teigen, "Luck, Envy, and

Gratitude: It Could Have Been Different," *Scandinavian Journal of Psychology* 38 (1997): 313–23.

38. Like the above, counterfactual thinking could also be displayed when comparing one's advantageous state with another's less fortunate circumstances.

39. Benefit-finding in the face of adversity is a coping strategy that has been documented in those suffering from serious medical conditions. See Glenn Affleck and Howard Tennen, "Constructing Benefits from Adversity: Adaptational Significance and Dispositional Underpinnings," *Journal of Personality* 64 (1996): 899–922.

40. In the self-help literature, codependency usually refers to a person who, in relationship with another, depends on the other's sickness. He or she also is dependent; hence the term *codependent*. I have several problems with this term. First, it is a very general statement, and it is frequently difficult to discern exactly which behaviors are most relevant. Second, it can be a harmful form of labeling that invites a stigma. Third, those who label others at times have their own issues and, as a consequence, the comment often says more about the one who is doing the labeling. Finally, the term tends to focus on the person rather than on the actual behavior that needs alteration. A more helpful approach, I think, is to focus specifically on the behavior itself. Thus, instead of saying, "You are codependent on him," a more useful comment could be: "I think you are encouraging her behavior by doing...."

41. Melanie Klein, *Envy and Gratitude* (New York: Basic Books, 1957), 19.

42. For a discussion of the "broaden and build" theory, see Barbara L. Fredrickson, "Positive Emotions" in *Handbook of Positive Psychology*, ed. C. R. Snyder and Shane J. Lopez (New York: Oxford University Press, 2002), 120–34. For the application of this theory to gratitude, see Barbara L. Fredrickson, "Gratitude, Like Other Positive Emotions, Broadens and Builds," in *The Psychology of Gratitude*, ed. Robert A. Emmons and Michael E. McCullough (New York: Oxford University Press, 2004), 145–66.

43. Barbara L. Fredrickson, "Gratitude, Like Other Positive Emotions, Broadens and Builds," 148.

44. Ibid., 152.

Chapter Four

1. Scott Turow, *Personal Injuries* (New York: Farrar, Straus and Giroux, 1999), 375.

2. Dan P. McAdams, "The Psychology of Life Stories," *Review of General Psychology* 5 (2001): 100–122.

3. William F. Buckley, Jr., *Let's Talk of Many Things: The Collected Speeches* (Roseville, CA: Prima Publishing, 2000), 336.

4. Ibid.

5. Quoted in Scott Sleek, "Wiesel Emphasizes Need to Thank the Elderly," *APA Monitor* 28 (October 1997): 23.

6. Mitch Albom, *Tuesdays with Morrie* (New York: Doubleday, 1997), 10.

7. Ibid., 190.

8. Ibid.

9. Quoted in Dan P. McAdams, "Gratitude in Modern Life: Its Manifestations and Development," in *Kindling the Science of Gratitude: A Symposium*, ed. Robert A. Emmons (Radnor, PA: The John Templeton Foundation, 2000), 2.

10. MSNBC, "Rediscovered Heroes," http://www.msnbc.com/news/662500.asp?Ocb=61724124 (retrieved November 25, 2001).

11. Quoted in Robert A. Emmons and Michael E. McCullough, "Counting Blessings Versus Burdens: An Experimental Investigation of Gratitude and Subjective Well-Being in Daily Life," *Journal of Personality and Social Psychology* 84 (2003): 377.

12. Michael E. McCullough, Jo-Ann Tsang, and Robert A. Emmons, "Gratitude in Intermediate Affective Terrain: Links of Grateful Moods to Individual Differences and Daily Emotional Experience," *Journal of Personality and Social Psychology* 86 (2004): 295–309.

13. I equate conscience with moral health. See Charles M. Shelton, *Achieving Moral Health* (New York: Crossroad Publishing, 2000).

14. For a fuller exploration of this virtue, see June Price Tangney, "Humility: Theoretical Perspectives, Empirical Findings and Directions for Future Research," *Journal of Social and Clinical Psychology* 19 (2000): 70–82.

15. Edmund Bergler, "Psychopathology of Ingratitude," *Diseases of the Nervous System* 6 (1945): 226.

16. For an overview of childhood moral development, see William Damon, *The Moral Child* (New York: The Free Press, 1988).

17. Jean Berko Gleason and Sandra Weintraub, "The Acquisition of Routines in Child Language," *Language in Society* 5 (1976): 129–36; and Jean Berko Gleason, Rivka Y. Perlmann, and Esther Blank Greif, "What's the Magic Word: Learning Language Through Politeness Routines," *Discourse Processes* 7 (1984): 493–502.

18. Sandra Graham, "Children's Developing Understanding of the Motivational Role of Affect: An Attributional Analysis," *Cognitive Development* 3 (1988): 71–88.

19. James A. Russell and Faye A. Paris, "Do Children Acquire Concepts for Complex Emotions Abruptly?" *International Journal of Behavioral Development* 17 (1994): 349–65.

20. Dan P. McAdams and Jack J. Bauer, "Gratitude in Modern Life: Its Manifestations and Development," in *The Psychology of Gratitude*, ed. Robert A. Emmons and Michael E. McCullough (New York: Oxford University Press, 2004), 89.

21. Ibid.

22. Charles M. Shelton, *Adolescent Spirituality* (New York: Crossroad Publishing, 1990), 29–120; and William Damon and Daniel Hart, *Self-Understanding in Childhood and Adolescence* (New York: Cambridge University Press, 1988).

23. Dan P. McAdams and Jack J. Bauer, "Gratitude in Modern Life: Its Manifestations and Development," 89–90.

24. For a thoughtful critique of spirituality's at times rather naive view of gratitude, see Edward C. Vacek, SJ, "Gift, God, Generosity, and Gratitude," in *Spirituality and Moral Theology: Essays from a Pastoral Perspective*, ed. James Keating (New York/Mahwah, NJ: Paulist Press, 2000), 81–125.

25. Ron Rosenbaum, *Explaining Hitler: The Search for the Origins of His Evil* (New York: Random House, 1998).

26. For a discussion of Hitler's numerous opportunities for gratitude in his life before World War II, see Ian Kershaw, *Hitler: 1889–1936: Hubris* (New York: Norton, 1998).

27. Karl E. Scheibe, *The Drama of Everyday Life* (Cambridge, MA; Harvard University Press, 2000), 209.

28. I have attempted to work out the criteria for a secular understanding of goodness. See Charles M. Shelton, "Gratitude: Considerations from a Moral Perspective," in *The Psychology of Gratitude*, ed. Robert A. Emmons and Michael E. McCullough (New York: Oxford University Press, 2004), 270–76.

29. This diversity of moral thinking is well illustrated in Alan Wolfe, *Moral Freedom: The Search for Virtue in a World of Choice* (New York: Norton, 2001).

30. Lawrence J. Walker and Russell C. Pitts, "Naturalistic Conceptions of Moral Maturity," *Developmental Psychology* 34 (1998): 403–19.

31. Of course, even though Christians find their sense of goodness rooted in the person and life of Jesus Christ, there is no getting around the fact that Christians differ as to how to apply the values and ideas of Jesus. We need only witness the diversity of beliefs among the Christian communities themselves, as well as the tensions and disagreements that exist within any one religious tradition. Nonetheless, there does exist general consensus that, in terms of broad principles, when using the life of Jesus as a moral reference point, Christians behave toward others in loving and compassionate ways, seek justice, and (in light of our discussion here) act gratefully.

Chapter Five

1. Josef Neuner, "Mother Teresa's Charism," *Review for Religious* 60 (2001): 481.

2. Edward Schillebeeckx, OP, *Jesus: An Experiment in Christology*, trans. Hubert Hoskins (New York: Vintage Books, 1981), 665.

3. I am grateful to John Ridgway, SJ, whose knowledge of scripture and insightful comments did much to enhance this section.

4. An informed and very readable introduction to discovering the life of Jesus is found in Daniel J. Harrington, SJ, *Jesus: A Historical Portrait* (Cincinnati: St. Anthony Messenger Press, 2007).

5. For an extended treatment of the Jewish perspective on gratitude, see Solomon Schimmel, "Gratitude in Judaism," in *The Psychology of Gratitude*, ed. Robert A. Emmons and Michael E. McCullough (New York: Oxford University Press, 2004), 37–57.

6. James Martin, SJ, "The Most Infallible Sign: Recovering Joy, Humor and Laughter in the Spiritual Life," *America* 196 (2007): 13–18.

7. Ibid.

8. David L. Fleming, SJ, "Jesus Our Redeemer: An Ignatian Perspective on Our Relationship with Our Redeeming God," *Jesuit* LXXXVII (Spring/Summer 2008): 11.

9. Joseph Ratzinger (Pope Benedict XVI), *Jesus of Nazareth*, trans. Adrian J. Walker (New York: Doubleday, 2007).

10. Sadly, some people have life histories whose predominant theme is guilt. Their behavior can be viewed as attempts to assuage guilt, or they engage in such actions as a means to incur guilt, thereby finding a means for self-punishment. Regardless of the motive, their actions tend to be habitual, and this invites chronic suffering. A second type of person apt to be attracted to a gratitude-in-suffering mode for unhealthy reasons is the compulsive caregiver. These individuals are uneasy with letting others care for them and seek to be the one doing the caring regardless of the personal cost. Needless to say, neither guilt nor compulsive caring has anything to do with Jesus' gratitude-in-suffering.

11. Interestingly, scientific study has shown that grateful people act in caring ways toward others even if such behavior proves "costly" to them. See Monica Y. Bartlett and David DeSteno, "Gratitude and Prosocial Behavior: Helping When It Costs You," *Psychological Science* 17 (2006): 319–25.

12. Quoted in Peter G. van Breemen, SJ, *Let All God's Glory Through* (New York/Mahwah, NJ: Paulist Press, 1995), 47.

13. Daniel Harrington, SJ, "The Word: Keeping the Memory of Jesus Alive," *America* 198 (2008): 46.

14. Though the "cost of gratitude" is central to any deeply felt gratitude and most certainly a defining feature of gratitude as a way of life, we must not idealize suffering. More specifically, there are some events in life that seem to defy any attempt at discovering a grateful sense. We find incomprehensible the cold-blooded murder of

a family member or dear friend. A child sexually or physically abused can spend a lifetime trying to compensate emotionally for such grievous wrong. The ravaging consequences of natural disasters leave us numb and overwhelmed. Other situations that appear far removed from gratitude are chronic irresolvable life stressors that deplete our psychic energies, such as being trapped in a job or irretrievably broken marriage that, for financial reasons, we cannot escape. Other examples might include an aging parent faithfully caring for an adult child who is developmentally disabled or an individual whose chronic and increasingly incapacitating illness leads to premature death. As we struggle with such experiences, we feel anything but gratitude. When gratitude does surface over some undefined *period of time*, it usually arises as some measure of thankfulness for one or more of the following: (a) acquiring self-insight, (b) considering "what if" situations that detail how the situation or incident could have been even more devastating, (c) finding solace in the kindnesses of others, (d) discovering inner strengths and talents that were unknown prior to the tragedy, and (e) drawing inspiration from the nobility of spirit displayed by others undergoing similar sufferings. At the very least, the gratitude we do develop helps to sustain us and proves hopeful in the midst of such affliction and torment.

15. William F. Buckley, Jr., *Let Us Talk of Many Things: The Collected Speeches* (Roseville, CA: Prima Publishing, 2000), 335.

16. Edward C. Vacek, SJ, "The Eclipse of the Love for God," *America* 174 (1996): 16.

17. Roy F. Baumeister, *Escaping the Self* (New York: Basic Books, 1990), 11–12.

18. From a historical perspective, there evolved a saying within Jesuit spirituality (attributed to St. Ignatius) that went something like the following: "Pray as if everything depends upon God and work as if everything depends upon you." The invitation to workaholism conveyed in this statement is obvious to anyone. As it turns out, more recent scholarship shows that St. Ignatius never made such a statement, and the one comment from which it could have derived actually means just the opposite! For a discussion of this issue see William A. Barry, SJ, and Robert G. Doherty, SJ, *Contemplatives in Action: The Jesuit Way* (New York/Mahwah, NJ: Paulist Press, 2002), 22–23.

19. Nathaniel M. Lambert, Frank D. Fincham, Scott R. Braithwaite, Steven M. Graham, and Steven R. H. Beach, "Can Prayer Increase Gratitude?" *Psychology of Religion and Spirituality* 1 (2009): 130–49.

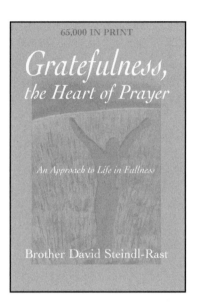

Gratefulness, The Heart of Prayer
An Approach to Life in Fullness
Brother David Steindl-Rast, OSB

A monk reflects on the many aspects of the spiritual life with the basic attitude of gratefulness.

"A true delight."—Henri J. M. Nouwen

0-8091-2628-1   Paperback

A 30 Day Retreat
A Personal Guide to Spiritual Renewal
William C. Mills

Ideal for a retreat, here are thirty brief meditations
on select scripture passages that are meaningful
to spiritual growth and fulfillment.

978-0-8091-4642-0   Paperback

Where the Hell Is God?

Richard Leonard, SJ; Foreword by James Martin, SJ

HiddenSpring

Combines professional insights along with the author's
own experience and insights to speculate on how
believers can make sense of their Christian faith
when confronted with tragedy and suffering.

978-1-58768-060-1   Paperback

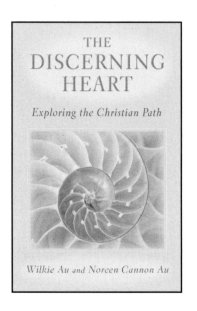

The Discerning Heart
Exploring the Christian Path
Wilkie Au and Noreen Cannon Au

Integrating the wisdom of Christian tradition and recent
psychological findings on effective decision-making,
this volume presents a view of Christian discernment
that honors the body-spirit unity of the person and the
broad and mysterious ways we can be led by the
Spirit of God in our life-choices.

0-8091-4372-0   Paperback

A Serenity Journal
Fifty-Two Weeks of Prayer and Gratitude
Rita Esposito Watson

A prayer journal based on 52 weeks of the year
in which persons can record their "thank you's,"
wishes or needs and miracles.

0-8091-3967-7   Paperback

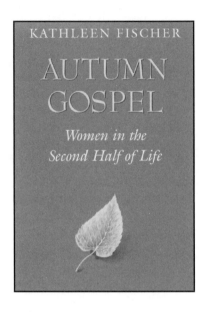

Autumn Gospel
Women in the Second Half of Life
Kathleen Fischer

Explores the spiritual dimensions of women's middle and
late years through the use of stories, experiences
and research from a variety of traditions and cultures.

0-8091-3581-7   Paperback

Overcoming Life's 7 Common Tragedies
Opportunities for Discovering God
Chris Benguhe

Reveals the positive potential of life's 7 most common catastrophes because sometimes the worst of times are the windows to the best.

978-0-8091-4391-7   Paperback

Enjoying Retirement
Living Life to the Fullest
Leonard Doohan

Offers practical advice to retirees while challenging
them to approach this period of life with fidelity
to the inner values of their hearts, so they
can truly live with purpose in later life.

978-0-8091-4635-2   Paperback

Spiritual Masters for All Seasons

Michael Ford

HiddenSpring

A blend of the spiritual and journalistic, this book
explores the outer characters and inner convictions
of the most inspirational figures of recent times.

978-1-58768-055-7   Paperback

Becoming Who You Are:
Insights on the True Self from
Thomas Merton and Other Saints
James Martin, SJ

HiddenSpring

By meditating on personal examples from the author's life,
as well as reflecting on the inspirational life and writings of
Thomas Merton, stories from the Gospels, as well as the lives
of other holy men and women (among them, Henri Nouwen,
Therese of Lisieux and Pope John XXIII) the reader will see
how becoming who you are, and becoming the person
that God created, is a simple path to happiness,
peace of mind and even sanctity.

1-58768-036-X   Paperback

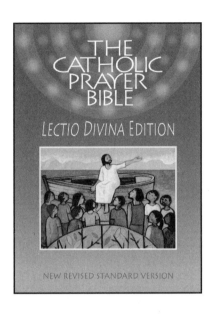

The Catholic Prayer Bible (NRSV)
Lectio Divina Edition
Paulist Press

An ideal Bible for anyone who desires to reflect on
the individual stories and chapters of just one, or even all,
of the biblical books, while being led to prayer
though meditation on that biblical passage.

978-0-8091-0587-8   Hardcover
978-0-8091-4663-5   Paperback